Walk!

Madeira

with

Ros & David Brawn

DISCOVERY WALKING GUIDES LTD

Walk! Madeira
First Edition published July 2006

Copyright © 2006

Published by
Discovery Walking Guides Ltd
10 Tennyson Close, Northampton NN5 7HJ,
England

Maps
Maps sections are taken from **Madeira Tour &
Trail Map** (Super-Durable Edition, ISBN 1-
904946-26-7) published by **Discovery Walking
Guides Ltd**. and re-scaled to 1:25,000 for each
walking route.

Photographs
All photographs in this book were taken by the
authors.

Front Cover Photographs

On the Levada da Serra (Walk 9)   Walk 6, 'Tea & Scones'

Western Funchal Grand   Portela Woodland Circular
Tour (Walk 1)   (Walk 25)

ISBN 1-904946-24-0
(978-1-904946-24-3)

Walk! Madeira
CONTENTS

THE WALKS

WALKS IN THE FUNCHAL REGION

WALKS IN THE CENTRAL (EAST) REGION

David and Ros Brawn lived and worked in England, Papua New Guinea and the Seychelles before settling some years ago in Tenerife. David's first published books were accountancy texts.

David and Ros have been walking and writing for Discovery Walking Guides since its beginnings in 1995, researching guides for most of the Canary Islands, the Balearic Islands, regions of the Spanish Mainland and Madeira.

In addition to the walking research, they have surveyed and mapped a number of these regions using satellite navigation equipment combined with cartographic software.

Considering themselves to be semi-permanent travellers, they divide their non-research time between Spain and Northampton, England.

David is a member of the British Cartographic Society.

David & Ros Brawn are joint authors of a number of publications including:

Sierra de Aracena - a Walk! Guidebook
Walk! Lanzarote
Walk! Tenerife
Walk! Menorca
Walk! Madeira

David is also the author of:
GPS The Easy Way

Acknowledgements

Our sincere thanks to all who have used our earlier Madeira walking publications, particularly those who have kept us informed of our errors and omissions and whose suggestions for further routes have been invaluable.

Madeira is a wonderful destination for walkers. Verdant flora, from meadow flowers up to magnificent tree specimens, clothes a landscape of mountains, great valleys, soaring cliffs and an upland plateau.

Funchal, as seen from Walk 2

Away from the sprawl of **Funchal**, settlements and hamlets cling to ridges and sit in valleys, their plots of vines, fruit trees and vegetables making ingenious use of fertile slopes, pockets and terraces.

Add in the comprehensive *levada* system and we have an island of walking experiences from gentle strolls right up to Alpine-style mountain challenges.

Whatever your level of walking fitness and ability, Madeira offers an exciting experience. It's easy to see why so many walkers return to this beautiful island year after year.

GEOGRAPHY & GEOLOGY

Although Portuguese, Madeira's nearest neighbours are the Spanish Canary Islands 400 kilometres away, and Morocco, some 600 kilometres distant. Massive volcanic activity under the Atlantic over 100 million years ago heaved **Madeira**, **Porto Santo** and the uninhabited **Ilhas Desertas** into being from the ocean floor. The volcanoes are long extinct and the effects of erosion and human activity have obscured all but a few craters (near **Fanal** and **Santo da Serra**), although what's thought to be an exposed volcanic 'bomb' can be seen above **Camacha** shopping (Walk 8, 'Camacha Shopping - Levada da Serra West - Bar Miranda' and Walk 9, 'Camacha - Levada da Serra East - Camacha'.

The principal island of Madeira extends to 57 kilometres east-west and 23 kilometres north-south, with an area of about 737 square kilometres. The central massif includes the great peaks of **Pico Ruivo** (1862 metres, climbed on Walk 18) with the summits of **Arieiro** and **Cidrão** not far behind at over 1800 metres, closely followed by the peaks of **Cedro**, **Casado**, **Grande** and **Ferreiro**.

Mountain views from Levada do Norte

The north coast boasts steep, high cliffs, but the highest of all is **Cabo Girão** on the south coast. Almost the entire coastline is rugged and scarped with virtually no beaches; those who crave a calm sandy cove must hop over to **Porto Santo**.

CLIMATE

In common with many mountainous islands, Madeira experiences numerous micro-climates within its broadly sub-tropical climate. Generally speaking, the north of the island is wetter and cloudier. than the south, while along the island's roughly west-east mountainous spine the weather is subject to rapid change and is often wild, windy, wet and cloudy - and occasionally, snowy. South of the spine the weather is generally more settled, sunnier and drier. **Funchal** has an annual average temperature of about 18.7°C while that of **Bica da Cana** is 9.3°C. You can expect an average of 90 wet days per year in **Funchal**, but 160 days in **Bica da Cana**, which also experiences, on average, 10 days on which snow falls and 15 days when it hails..

Clouds often gather and winds increase as the day progresses, so if planning long or high level routes, it's best to start early. The daytime temperature frequently reaches 30°C during July and August, with daytime highs of 16-17°C from December to March. Wettest months for most areas are October to March.

THE LEVADAS
Levada da Serra (Walks 8&9)

Although irrigation channels are not unique to Madeira, the island undoubtedly boasts some of the world's finest examples. There are now over 1400 kilometres of *levada*s on the island, and new channels are still being constructed. As soon as the early settlers began clearing terraced pockets of land on which to raise crops, they needed to guide the rain waters to these *poios*, and so the *levadas* began.

Levada da Ribeira da Janela (Walk 35)

It's thought that the first attempts in the 15th century were made from lengths of wood, gradually replaced with more durable and watertight stone channels. Newer versions are made from reinforced concrete.

Most slope gently - almost imperceptibly in some cases - as they follow the natural contours of the terrain, providing ideal walking where the accompanying paths allow. Where the shape of the land gets in the way, tunnels have been pushed through to take the channels.

In the last decades of the 20th century hydroelectric power stations harnessing the power of 100 kilometres of new high altitude *levadas* were built, now providing some 20% of the islands power.

From the walker's point of view, the *levadas* not only provide memorable and beautiful walking experiences, they open up otherwise impenetrable regions of the island.

PLANT LIFE

Eucalyptus

The island's name means 'wood', so named by early settlers who found it almost covered by great forests, mostly of laurisilva, similar to that still thriving on La Gomera in the Canary Islands.

Only pockets of this ancient laurel woodland remain, as the wood was used as timber, and lower woodlands were burnt to release land for farming and pastures.

Mimosa

Newer forests of pine, acacia (also called mimosa), eucalyptus and oak now occupy much of the laurisilva's former territory.

Heathland at Bica da Cana

The climate and fertility of Madeira ensures a dazzling range of trees, shrubs, flowers and fruits, although some regions support little more than rough grasslands and heather, such as the high meadows of **Paúl da Serra** (Walks 29 & 30, 'Bica da Cana (east)' and 'Bica da Cana' (west)), while the highest peaks consist largely of bare rock.

The dramatic **São Lourenço** peninsula to the east (Walk 19, **'São Lourenço**

One of many banana plantations

Peninsula') is a surprising contrast to the rest of the island, formed mostly of variously coloured rock with scant, low-level vegetation.

Land once occupied by native woodland now supports a wide range of crops including bananas, grapes, passionfruit sugar cane and papaya, as well as potatoes, onions, tomatoes, beans of various types and brassicas.

Cropping trees such as lemon, orange, chestnut and walnut thrive, and cut flowers have become an important export.

Strelizia regina

Introduced plants including the hydrangea, strelizia and agapanthus have become naturalised with such ease that it's as if they've always thrived on the island, flourishing alongside the beautiful blue echium, native to Madeira,

The streets of **Funchal** are softened by avenues of flowering trees, including the distinctive blue-mauve jacaranda in spring.

One of Funchal's Jacaranda trees

Echium

Flower lovers should try to fit in visits to some of some of Madeira's many gardens. See the appendices for contact details.

When to Walk

Bearing in mind the island's climate, and that it is extremely lush and green, it follows that you can expect wet days on any visit. If you want to do high altitude routes, it's advisable to go when it is drier, from April to September. Some *levada* walks are popular even in the rain, and frequently offer shade during the hotter months; for example, the 'walking motorway' route from **Ribeiro Frio** to **Portela** (Walk 13, 'Portela Bound').

Go prepared for sun, wind or rain, whatever type of route you choose and whatever the time of year. (see 'Walking Equipment' on page 21).

Trails and Paths

Terrain on the routes varies widely. Some *levada* walks, although long, are on flat, easy paths with negligible ascents and descents; other *levada* routes may require far more concentration on narrow paths, perhaps with sheer drops or on slippery, poor surfaces.

An easy, typically verdant levada path

Mountain routes are typically rocky and dusty, often with loose steep sections and occasionally requiring a bit of scrambling using hands and feet.

The terrain on Walk 18, Pico do Ruivo

Our routes crossing mountain pastures such as Walk 22, 'Levada do Caniçal East' and Walk 23, 'Old Trail to Caniçal', in the east of the island, follow faint trails often obscured by vegetation.

Walk 23, on a faint trail

The steep nature of the island means that many downhill routes (for example, Walk 3 'Bom Succeso - The Route to Town'), put a lot of strain on knees that are not used to it.

The island's authorities have recently erected new signs at the starts/ends of the most popular routes and at route intersections, such as at the **Lamaceiros Posto Florestal**.

In some cases, though, the trail soon disappears only a few metres from the start point, hopefully only because the powers that be have not yet got around to clearing these routes, but intend to do so.

Walk information at Levada da Ribeira da Janela

Preparation
Be prepared - read through the walk description before you set out, and take note of the information bar for each route. If you are new to walking on Madeira, start with a shorter, easier route.

Exertion ratings range from 1 (easy) to 5 (strenuous); these are inevitably subjective - our 'strenuous' would be 'average' for those fitter (or younger) than we are. The time taken for each route is our own recorded time, and does not include stops for taking photos or refreshments. It's advisable to try one or our shorter routes first in order to compare your pace with ours, then adjust the time you need to allow accordingly. Distance is shown in kilometres, and ascents and descents in metres. Vertigo risk ranges from 0 (no risk) to 3 (high vertigo risk). Note that the vertigo risk often applies to only a short section of the route, although if you're a sufferer, this could feel like the longest few metres you've ever walked.

See the symbols ratings guide on page 15.

Safety
Do take safety seriously. If you find a route made impassable by, for example, a landslide, then turn back. Attempting to find your own way through can be highly risky. Take note of local weather forecasts, and remember that weather changes happen swiftly on mountainous islands, especially at altitude. Start out early and plan to finish well before dusk. Let someone know (at your

hotel, for example) where you plan to walk, and if possible walk with a companion. Bear in mind that mobile phones may not always work in remote parts of the island. Go properly equipped with an up to date map and guide book; we'd recommend a GPS and/or compass also. Clothing, including footwear, must be up to the job. Advice on these and on other essentials to put in your pack are listed in 'Walking Equipment' on page 21.

GETTING AROUND

Car hire is good value, but many of the minor roads demand that drivers have nerves of steel. However, the **Via Rápida**, the major roads and the incredible road tunnels make reaching the corners of the island far quicker and easier than even a decade ago, and more roads and tunnels are constantly under construction.

But if you want to leave the driving licence at home and relax, we recommend you make use of the excellent bus services. Bus journeys are an adventure, when you'll admire not only the high-up views of the scenery, but also the aplomb of the bus drivers who hurl their vehicles around impossible bends hanging over dizzying drops.

Many of the walks in this book can be accessed by bus (see each walk's introduction for details) and there are special tickets that make this good value, fun travel even cheaper (see appendices). We also recommend the Madeira Bus & Touring Map (pub. Discovery Walking Guides ISBN 1-904946-09-7 £2.50), an invaluable aid for bus users and car drivers alike.

Taxis are another option at reasonable cost. See the appendices at the back of this book for taxi phone numbers.

A novel form of transport are the cable cars or *teleféricos*. There are two routes, between **Funchal** sea front and **Monte**, and between **Babosas** and the **Jardim Botânico** in **Bom Sucesso**, **Funchal**. You can buy one-way or return tickets, so could combine a bus one way/cable car the other for a sightseeing day out, or could add in one or more of our walks in the area (see Walks 2-5).

Teleférico 2 at Babosas

THINGS TO DO (OTHER THAN WALKING)

Given the island's climate, it follows that you might experience a couple of days on which you'd prefer not to walk; in any case, it's a good idea to do something different for a day and give those muscles and knees a rest.

Madeira is justifiably famous for its wines, even to the extent of being mentioned by William Shakespeare. There are a number of wine lodges and cellars, and plenty of grape vineyards, some of which you'll see while on our walking routes. If you would like to find out more, there are organised visits to some of the most famous wine producers' premises with the inevitable tastings and encouragements to buy.

Madeira's markets are worth a visit, especially the one in **Funchal** which is a riot of flowers, fruits and vegetables, fish and handicrafts.

Take a cable car ride - there are two *teleféricos* to try, one from the eastern end **Funchal** sea front to Monte, and the other linking the **Madeira Botanical Garden** at **Bom Sucesso** with **Babosas**.

Go adventuring on the excellent bus services. As well as accessing many of our walking routes, they make great sightseeing days out - and at pocket money prices. You can buy special multi-trip tickets that reduce the costs even further. Ask in the bus kiosks along **Funchal** sea front, and get hold of a Madeira Bus & Touring Map.

See the Appendices at the back of this book for contact details for other activities such as fishing, bird watching and climbing. Tourist Offices can provide details of the island's many museums.

SYMBOLS RATING GUIDE

 our rating for effort/exertion:-
1 very easy **2** easy **3** average
4 energetic **5** strenuous

approximate **time** to complete a walk (compare your times against ours early in a walk) - does not include stopping time

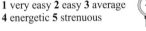 approximate walking **distance** in kilometres

 approximate **ascents/descents** in metres (N=negligible)

 circular route

linear route

 figure of eight route

 risk of **vertigo**
0 = nil 1 = low
2 = medium 3 = high

 refreshments (may be at start or end of a route only)

Walk descriptions include:

- timing in minutes, shown as (40M)
- compass directions, shown as (NW)
- heights in metres, shown as (1355m)
- GPS waypoints, shown as (Wp.3)

Notes on the text
Place names are shown in **bold text**, except where we refer to a written sign, when they are enclosed in single quotation marks. Local or unusual words are shown in *purple italics*, and are explained in the accompanying text or in the glossary.

WALKS IN THE NORTH-WEST REGION

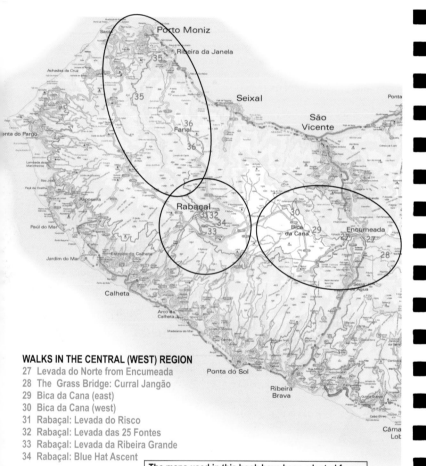

WALKS IN THE CENTRAL (WEST) REGION

The maps used in this book have been adapted from:
   Madeira Tour & Trail Super-Durable Map
       4th edition ISBN 1-904946-26-7
and
       Madeira Bus& Touring Map
          ISBN 1-904946-09-7
published by:
       Discovery Walking Guides Ltd.
          10 Tennyson Close
             Northampton
               NN5 7HJ
               England

WALKS IN THE CENTRAL (EAST) REGION
11 Balcões
12 Ribeiro Frio Circular Tour
13 Portela Bound
14 A Wizardly Tower: Pico do Suna
15 Portela - Santo da Serra
16 Levada do Castelejo
17 The Green Pool (Caldeiro Verde - nearly)
18 Pico Ruivo
(Notes) Pico do Arieiro: A Head for Heights

WALKS IN THE EAST
19 São Lourenço Peninsula
20 Levada do Caniçal (west)
21 Pico do Facho
22 Levada do Caniçal East
23 The Old Trail to Caniçal
24 Boca do Risco
25 Portela Woodland Circular
26 All Weather Strolling: Machico - Ribeira Seca

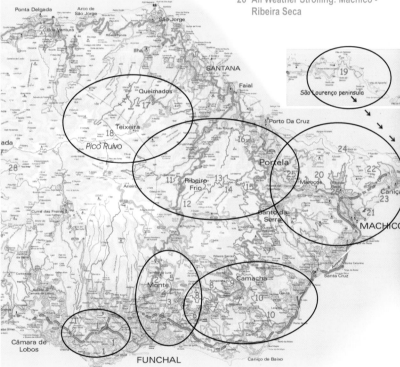

WALKS IN THE FUNCHAL REGION
1 Western Funchal Grand Tour
2 Terreiro da Luta: Body & Soul
3 Bom Sucesso: The Route To Town
4 Curral Romeiros to Monte/Babosas: The Traditional Route
5 'New' Levada dos Tornos: Monte/Babosas to Curral Romeiros
6 Tea & Scones: Romeiros - Jasmin Tea House
7 Jasmin Tea House - Camacha Centre
8 Camacha (shopping) -Levada da Serra West - Bar Miranda
9 Camacha (shopping) - Levada da Serra East - Camacha
10 Levada do Caniço

The map sections used in this book have been taken from Madeira Tour & Trail Super-Durable Map (ISBN 1-904946-26-7) published by Discovery Walking Guides Ltd. All map sections have been re-sized to a scale of 1:25.000 and are aligned so that north is at the top of the page. In the interests of clarity adjoining and inter-linking walking routes have been deleted from the map sections for each specific walking route. Waypoint positions, and numbers, refer to the walking route that the map section is illustrating.

Madeira Tour & Trail Super-Durable Map is a 1:40,000 scale full colour map. For more information on DWG publications, write to DWG Ltd, 10 Tennyson Close, Northampton NN5 7HJ, England, or visit:

www.walking.demon.co.uk   www.dwgwalking.co.uk

Legend for Map Sections

ALTITUDE & HEIGHTS

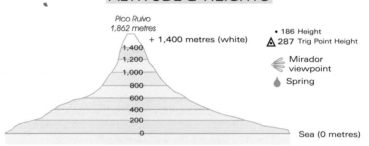

ROADS & SYMBOLS

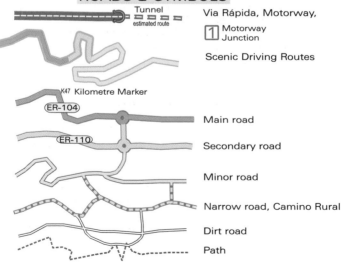

🌷 Gardens	🚠 Teleférico Cable Car		Urban area
🗼 Tower	🎆 Lighthouse	⛪ Chapel	⛪ Church
P Parking	🍴 Bar/Rest	🏨 Hotel	⛽ Petrol ♨ Picnic area ⚡ Pylon
🏟 Sports Ground	⛺ Camping		✚ Cemetery
✦ Wind Turbine	ⓘ Information	⚲ Vertiginous section of route	

⛬ Forest House, Posto Florestal *Rib* Ribeira, River *Lev* Levada, Canal

WALKING ROUTES

Walk! Madeira Walking Routes (Red)

GPS Waypoints
see text & Waypoint Lists

14 🚶 19 13

Alternative walking routes and other published walking routes (Green)

USING GPS ON MADEIRA

Walk! Madeira walking routes include GPS Waypoints where there is good GPS reception. These waypoints refer to specific locations, and/or specific navigation choices, along the walking route. A full GPS Waypoint list is provided for each route, except where GPS reception is poor. Map sections to illustrate each walking route are specially adapted from our Madeira Tour & Trail Super-Durable Map 4th Edition and we have endeavoured to show as many Waypoints as possible on these sections, but even so on some routes not all waypoints are shown on the map section, in the interests of clarity.

All GPS Waypoints quoted in Walk! Madeira were recorded while researching the routes and are subject to the general considerations as to the accuracy of GPS units in the location concerned. To use these GPS Waypoints, remember to set your GPS Datum to WGS84; this is the default datum for most handheld GPS units. Using the wrong datum can result in significant errors in location.

GPS Waypoints are given in Latitude/Longitude co-ordinates; e.g. start of route 25 at **Bar/Rest Miradouro da Portela** is Wp.1 32° 44.8338N (Latitude) 16° 49.5426W (Longitude). All waypoints are quoted in the WGS84 datum coordinates. Using your GPS in the WGS84 datum will ensure that you co-ordinate with these waypoints and with positions on the Madeira Tour & Trail Super-Durable Map 4th edition.

Waypoints are quoted in Latitude/Longitude co-ordinates. For your GPS to be directly compatible with the GPS Waypoints and the Madeira Tour & Trail Super-Durable Map 4th edition, you should set the 'Location Format' of your GPS to 'hddd° .mm.mmm'; then the reading of your GPS with datum set to WGS84 directly correlates to waypoints quoted in this book and the co-ordinates on the Tour & Trail Map.

GPS Waypoints are approximate positions, and while we quote positions to 0.0001 minutes of arc in practice 0.0100 minutes of arc is an acceptable standard of accuracy. This level of accuracy assumes that you have reception from 4 or more satellites giving you '3D GPS Location'. Note that on the map sections for each walk the GPS Waypoint number is placed alongside the walking route for clarity, while the 'leg' from the number shows the location to which it refers.

Madeira presents a number of problems for GPS users. Many walking routes are along *levadas* which traverse steep slopes and cliffs where 'mountain shadowing' can severely reduce the number of satellites available. When walking through wooded terrain the bulk of the tree trunks can cut out satellite signals, often giving intermittent '3D GPS Location'. Even where you appear to have full satellite reception, it could be that you are receiving some reflected signals; this can often happen when close to cliff faces or amongst buildings. Locations which are particularly prone to poor GPS reception include the square in **Monte** (those big plane trees), Walk 5 on the vertiginous section of the *levada*, Walks 12 and 13 on the **Levada do Furado**, Walks 31, 32 & 34 routes from **Rabaçal** forest house, Walk 35 on the final sections of the route before the tunnel.

Of course, there are times when GPS is of no use at all for navigation. These include in tunnels and if your batteries run out (always carry spares). If you are a GPS user then you should consider purchasing our Personal Navigator Files CD which contains all the GPS Tracks and Waypoints for ALL of the routes which appear in ALL of DWG's Walk! Series of guide books (see the list of destinations covered below),, along with GPSU software and sample walking route for each of our destinations in UK and Europe. Once you have inputted GPS Waypoints by hand for a walking route, you'll immediately understand that £9.99 for our latest PNFs CD so that you load GPS information into your GPS unit in seconds is a very good investment; the CD also confirms DWG as 'Leaders in Walking Navigation at Home & Abroad'.

See our websites for more information on the latest version of our Personal Navigator Files CD.

Conventional 'Map & Compass' navigators who have read this far should also note that many sections of Madeira are magnetic so making any quotations as to the 'deflection/deviation from True North', subject to just where you are on the island. For this reason we do not quote any deflection/deviation from True North on our Tour & Trail Map.

Personal Navigator Files (PNFs).
Edited versions of all the GPS tracks and waypoints compiled during our research are available as PNFs on our Personal Navigator Files CD version 3.02. GPS Utility Special Edition software is included on the PNFs CD, enabling the user to load track and waypoint information direct to their GPS unit via a PC. In addition to **Madeira** the PNFs CD version 3.02 contains the GPS tracks and waypoints for **Mallorca West**, **Mallorca North & Mountains**, **Menorca**, **La Gomera**, **La Palma**, **Tenerife**, **Lanzarote**, **Sierra de Aracena**, **Alpujarras**, **Axarquia**, **Andorra**, and the full **Walk! UK** series of guide books covering **Lake District North**, **Lake District South**, **Yorkshire Dales (North & Central)**, **South Pennines**, **Peak District South**, **Brecon Beacons**, **South Downs**, **Dorset**, **Dartmoor** and **Exmoor**.

The PNFs CD version 3.02 is available from Discovery Walking Guides Ltd at £9.99 including postage.

Confused by GPS?
If you are confused by talk of GPS, but are interested in how this modern navigational aid could enhance your walking enjoyment, then simply seek out a copy of GPS The Easy Way, the UK's best selling GPS manual. Written in an easy to read, lively, style and lavishly illustrated, GPS The Easy Way takes you through all aspects of GPS usage from absolute basics up to GPS Expert and debunking the myths about GPS along the way; an essential purchase for anyone thinking of buying a GPS.

"A compass points north" but
"A GPS tells you where you are, where you have been, and can show you where you want to go."
"Ask not 'What is GPS?' - ask 'What can GPS do for me?' "

GPS The Easy Way £4.99 is available from bookshops and post free from:
Discovery Walking Guides Ltd.
10 Tennyson Close
Northampton NN5 7HJ
www.walking.demon.co.uk & www.dwgwalking.co.uk

WALKING EQUIPMENT

Reading the postings on uk.rec.walking internet news group, it is obvious that walkers are very interested in the clothing and equipment used by other walkers. For some this interest borders on obsession, with heated debates over walking poles, boots versus sandals, GPS versus 'map and compass' navigation etc etc. Walking magazines are packed with clothing and equipment reviews, opinions and adverts, but few walking guide books give more than a cursory mention to recommended clothing and equipment. At the risk of upsetting some walking fundamentalists, here is a brief rundown on what we've used on Madeira.

Backpack
A 25-30 litre day pack should easily cope with all the equipment you think you will need for a day's walking. A design with plenty of outside pockets to give easy access to frequently used items, such as ½ litre water bottles, is a good starting point. Well padded straps will spread the load and a waist strap will stop the pack moving about on the more adventurous routes. A ventilated back panel will help clear sweat on hot days and tough routes; a design with a stand-off frame is best for ventilation and worth the small increase in weight. Do spend time adjusting the straps so that you get the most comfortable fit.

As an alternative to traditional backpack designs, you might find the cyclist's packs produced by Nikko, and similar companies, a good compromise of stand-off frame, capacity, pockets and weight.

Footwear
Do not compromise on your footwear. While there are many comfortable paths on the island, a lot of the walking is on hard rock, usually uneven. Whether you choose boots, shoes or sandals (tough, rugged, walking sandals

such as Merrells), they must be up to the task. You will need a hard sole with plenty of grip and a well padded foot-bed. David's favourites are a pair of Bestard boots that he picked up at their factory shop on Mallorca. Worn with thick mountain socks, these boots have done everything I have asked of them. (Calzados Bestard, C/. Estación 40-42 Lloseta)

Whichever footwear you choose, do make sure that you have covered plenty of kilometres in them before coming to Madeira.

Sun Protection
Always carry a comfortable sun hat, also useful should it rain. Choose a design that gives you plenty of shade, is comfortable to wear, and stays on your head in windy conditions. You will be spending several hours a day outdoors and sunburnt ears (and neck) are both painful and embarrassing. Sunglasses and high-factor sun cream are highly recommended.

Water & Food
Always carry as much water as you think you might drink. A couple of ½ litre bottles, a few pence each from local shops, is the minimum, and add another couple of litres for more demanding routes. Even on shorter routes, I would advise that you carry some survival rations. While some routes are well equipped with 'tipico' bars these may not be open when you need them, so survival rations of chocolate bars and the like can provide welcome comfort.

Medical Kit
Antiseptic wipes, antiseptic cream, plasters and bandage are supplemented by lip salve, which can seem like a life saver in hot dry conditions. Also include tweezers, which you will soon appreciate if you catch a splinter or cactus spine, and a whistle to attract attention if you get into difficulties.

Navigation
Do not compromise - buy the best guide book and the best map, and carry them with you. A compass is useful to orientate yourself at the start of a route and for general directions, but a GPS unit is far more useful - see Using GPS on Madeira on P.19.

Clothing
Choose loose comfortable clothing and add a lightweight waterproof jacket to your back pack; Madeira is famous for both sunshine and copious rainfall. Pack extra layers, especially when walking at higher altitudes.

Other Equipment
You won't want to be carrying excess weight during your walking, especially on the longer routes with major ascents/descents. Digital cameras weigh far less than their film equivalents, and a monocular is half the weight of a pair of binoculars. Secateurs might seem an unusual choice of walking equipment, but they can be useful on some routes, and if a route includes a tunnel section, you'll need a torch. A mobile phone, and money (refreshments, taxis, public telephones, drinks machines etc.) are also recommended. Don't forget batteries for your GPS and torch.

Levada dos Piornais, our very first Madeira walk many years ago, was dropped when our early guides evolved into 35 Madeira Walks. Now we're back on this delightful *levada*, this time all the way into the **Socorridos Valley** with its exciting tunnels before a slogging ascent takes us up to **Pinheiro das Voltas**, and on upwards to the **Levada do Curral** where we take another of our old routes back into town on a little-known *levada* before dropping down through the streets to our start point, then down to the hotel district (**Monumental Lido/Eden Mar**). If you're based in the hotel district in **Funchal**, there's no better introduction to the delights of Madeira walking.

Access on Foot:
From the **Monumental Lido** take **Caminho da Casa Branca** uphill until you reach **Caminho da Nazare** where you turn uphill again, even steeper this time, until you emerge from between the walled houses into the open with the football ground on your right and our start point on your left.

Access by Bus:
Take town bus N°45 to **Nazare** from the centre and ask for **Levada dos Piornais**.

> **Extension**
> Add a country stroll to our route by simply following the open *levada* from Wp.29 out into the countryside and on through **Ribeira do Arvoredo** to the **Socorridos Valley**, a traditional *levada* path until railings protect you from the drop into the **Socorridos** at which point we suggest you turn round and return.

Access by Car:
There's on-street parking near the start of the route and at the football ground .

Almost opposite the N°45 bus-stop, we go down the green-railed steps (Wp.1 0M) onto the **Levada dos Piornais** path to stroll westward against the water flow with the hotel district laid out below us on the left. Green handrails guard the path until the next steps up to the road (Wp.2 3M) after which we continue above a small drop to cross a street (Wp.3 5M) then rejoin the *levada*, now paved. After the paving runs out we need to step carefully as we pass above overgrown plots and an old *lavadeiro* (Wp.4 11M) laundry area, remembering to always stop to look at the views.

Even this early in the route, the *levada* belongs to a rural world, quite different to that of the housing areas close by and the crowded hotel district below us. A dirt path takes us over a short section where the water channel is covered, before crossing a concrete lane by house N°70 (Wp.5 14M); despite the building boom below us, our route takes us past abandoned plots dotted with old cottages such as N°84 which sits above us in sharp contrast to the apartments beside the channel. A *tipico* blue shack (Wp.6) marks the end of the apartments and we are back onto the *levada* wall above grape vines.

Levada dos Piornais gradually swings right bringing the massive sea cliff of **Cabo Girão** into view, as we come onto 'bonging' slabs covering the water channel before tackling a section with an unprotected drop; use the inland *levada* wall, or both walls, if this section worries you. More 'bonging' slabs

Cabo Girão comes into view

bring us to a water-change point (Wp.7 25M) above a new development before block walling takes away the view as we curve round to emerge on a cobbled and tarmac street (Wp.8 29M); across it, we continue on the *levada*, passing between housing and onto a 'more main' road (Wp.9). Over the road below the Electricidade building we go down a concrete driveway signed 'Levada dos Piornais' to regain the paved water channel and head out amongst banana plantations.

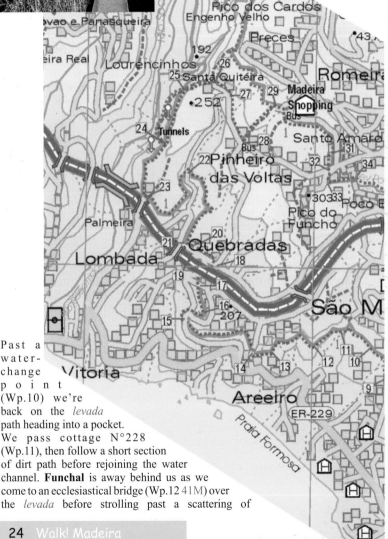

Past a water-change point (Wp.10) we're back on the *levada* path heading into a pocket. We pass cottage N°228 (Wp.11), then follow a short section of dirt path before rejoining the water channel. **Funchal** is away behind us as we come to an ecclesiastical bridge (Wp.12 41M) over the *levada* before strolling past a scattering of

The ecclesiastical bridge at Wp.12

crumbling cottages and modern houses to a strange mini-bridge over our route (Wp.13). Ducking under it, we're on a concrete access for the *levada*-side houses; across a cobbled *vereda* (Wp.14), tall railings protect us from a minor drop to the cultivated plots. 'Currasa das Herreras' is signed left as we come back onto paving running between a block wall on our left and a prickly pear plantation right; occasional slabs are missing on this section so make sure you don't step into the holes! We emerge on a street (Wp.15 59M) and cross it (on town bus route N°2) to continue on the paved channel beside grape vines and modern cottages.

The water goes underground while we follow a cobbled street round the head of the valley before going up steps (Wp.16) to rejoin the paved *levada* alongside some impressive rock walling, Madeira's equivalent of a dry-stone wall but on a grand scale. Approaching houses, we come to an unusual 'taxi' sign at **Familia Barros** and step up to the road (Wp.17 64M) with a T-junction where 'Levada dos Piornais' is signed left on the **Caminho dos Quebradas Baixo**; served by town bus N°2. We stroll up to a crossroads (Wp.18) to swing left past a tiny café/bar and access roads to the **Via Rápida** until, by the school (Wp.19), we take a diversion uphill for refreshments at **Snack Bar Santa Rita** (Wp.20 72M) being remodelled at June 2006.

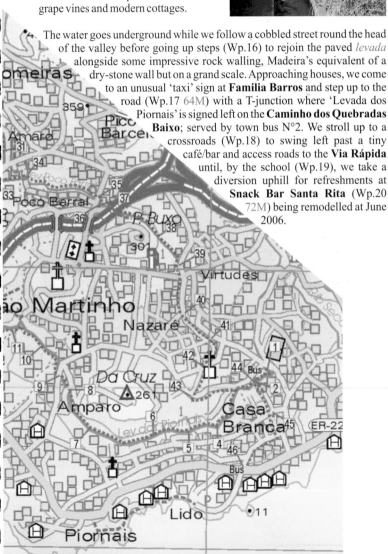

Here endeth our first-ever published Madeiran walk - but today, rather than bus back to **Funchal**, we continue onto our second tranche with the promise of some extreme excitement! To begin this second stage, we take our original stroll round a banana valley but follow it with some of the most dramatic walking you'll see anywhere; high vertigo warning, but if you can overcome this, then you're in for an experience!

From **Snack Bar Santa Rita** (Wp.20 0M) we stroll back down to the 'main' street (Wp.19) to turn right downhill. In 90 metres, as the street swings right downhill, we find the **Levada dos Piornais** (signed) on our right (Wp.21 3M) where we take to the broad paving which covers the rushing water.

Banana plantations after Wp.21

Banana plantations dotted with houses cover the valley on our left while above us modern houses look out over the Atlantic Ocean; views that repay the 'pedestrian only' access. Our 'bonging' progress on the paving brings us to cross the valley's access road (Wp.22 11M; town bus Nº16A) before continuing on the paved *levada* to the mouth of the banana valley (Wp.23 19M) at a bridge over the **Via Rápida**, water-change point and a faded signboard; this is where our original stroll turned back, but today we're up for some excitement.

Above the **Via Rápida**'s magnificent bridge, the **Levada dos Piornais** turns up the **Socorridos Valley**, becoming an open channel with railed *levada* path after house Nº541. There's an unprotected 50 metre section where the rails are broken away; if in doubt about your safety either walk on the inside of the channel or with one foot each side of it until the rails resume.

Turning into the Socorridos Valley

Views up the **Socorridos Valley** are superb despite the rock-crushing plant down below - but at all times concentrate on the narrow path and 'Stop to look at the view' - as the green railings bring us to the start of the infamous tunnels (Wp.24 29M); we've already been treated to quite an exhibition of water engineering, but this tunnel section exceeds even the highest expectations.

If you doubt your ability to traverse the tunnels, then take the alternative concrete steps for a knee-jarring descent to the valley floor and then a slogging stepped ascent up to the far end of the tunnels, but if you've come this far . . . .

Entering the first tunnel requires crawling on all fours under the low arch, and taking care straightening up after the arch (bumped head) before coming out onto an open section where the *levada* seems to be built on thin air.

We were concentrating too much to take notes but I remember short tunnels linked by seemingly impossible sections of *levada* (all railed) and then one section where the paving is topped with rock where I edged away from the drop into the valley to find that the water channel had left the cliff leaving a body-sized slit to drop through where I thought the cliff would be.

Time expands in conditions like this so I was grateful to exit the last tunnel and with the help of the railings for balance come along to the stepped path (Wp.25 37M) up from the valley floor for a good sit down; Ros meanwhile had almost danced through the experience and was so excited she wanted to go back and do it again, only stopped by walkers following us! Take your choice, but if you can do the tunnels you won't forget the experience.

Levada dos Piornais winds its way up the **Socorridos Valley** as we take the uphill concrete stair for an energy sapping climb to a house (Wp.26 46M) where we find we've been climbing the **Verada do Pico do Lombada**, to turn right on a concrete track. An easy stroll - at last - takes us along to a street coming up the valley (Wp.27) where we go left for a steady climb up past the houses, the gradient increasing before we come to a junction (Wp.28 54M) in **Pinheiro das Voltas** with a bar on the corner. We could continue ahead to connect with our return route but it's·a busy road with no pavement, so better to turn left uphill at the bar on the **Trevassa do Pinheiro das Voltas**. It's a steep climb up past houses on the traditional paved track before we come up to the **Levada do Curral** (Wp.29 63M) at the border between town and country.

At this point you could take our country stroll extension (see the information box at the start of this description) or you could bus back to town from Madeira Shopping on the N°08, 16 or 50 services.

Turning right (E) we follow the paved water channel along a cul-de-sac to a small roundabout (Wp.30) sitting below the monument to Mammon that is **Madeira Shopping**, topped with an extravagantly large specimen of Agave plasticana. Redevelopment means that the *levada* now runs under the pavement which we follow (E and then S) until we can go down steps (Wp.31) onto a access lane beside the water channel. A short stroll takes us to and across the busy **Caminho do Poço Barral**; the road that comes up from the **Pinheiro dos Voltas** junction (Wp.32 74M). If you fancy a break then the **Bruno Bar** sits just below where we cross the 'main' road, quite the best bar in this area.

Across the busy road, we take the quiet **Caminho do Pico do Funcho** tarmac lane to pass the tiny **Levada do Pico do Funcho** off on our right and **Bar**

The Vereda da Levada do Poço Barral at Wp.33

Mariano after which we need to look for the **Vereda da Levada do Poço Barral** (Wp.33 76M) on our left; signed but easily missed.

Following the water on the *levada* wall between banana and garden plots, we pass houses accessed from the path before crossing a tarmac lane (Wp.34) and a parking area. Continuing on the paved **Vereda da Levada do Poço Barral**, we pass more houses and garden plots as the *levada* starts to rush downhill - beware of missing slabs - to a filtration point beside a main street (Wp.35 87M).

Turning right, we head downhill, carefully crossing the road, towards the **São Martinho** cemetery to take the first left (Wp.36) by a bar onto the **Travesa do Mocho** to follow the water channel again along to the end of the cul-de-sac (Wp.37) where we take concrete steps to walk below the levada channel. Steel steps take us up onto the pedestrian bridge over the **Via Rápida**, the far end held together with scaffolding poles and planks (June 2006), to come alongside a military camp. Now we have an elevated stroll on the covered channel with superb views over **Funchal**, until our path ends at the head of concrete steps (Wp.38 97M). Originally the *levada* channel was open here, revealing a surging torrent heading steeply down alongside the stair, but it is now covered and quiet as we head steeply down to emerge, along with the water, on an access road. Again we follow the fast flowing water down the road to the **Rua do Sao Martinho** junction where the gradient eases and we pass a street off to our left before dropping down between houses to a main road (Wp.39 102M) at the bottom of **Rua do Ninho** where the foaming *levada* disappears underground.

Another careful crossing, this time of the **Caminho do São Martinho** main road, brings us onto the **Pavelleo do Cab** to stroll over a crest before passing the **Quinta da Bella Vista** (Wp.40) as we head downhill to a junction (Wp.41 110M) where we continue on **Pavello do Cab** to swing right in front of a school and come onto an incongruous short stretch of dual carriageway in front of the modern church at **Nazare** (Wp.42 113M) with its tall clock tower. Going either to the left of the church on an alleyway, or right on a street which the alleyway joins, we walk through housing (SW) to come onto a wider 'main' road (Wp.43 117M). If you wonder why we're wriggling through **Nazare'**s housing, you soon find out as we swing left downhill to sweeping views over **Funchal** and the Atlantic Ocean; there are even picnic tables set beneath shady trees to take a break in this unexpected setting. A gentle downhill stroll on the broad pavement brings us down to walk above the **Levada dos Piornais** to its access steps (Wp.2/Wp.44 127M).

To return to the hotel district we take the access steps across the *levada* to walk down a cul-de-sac of modern housing, then cross the 'new' road (Wp.45) onto another cul-de-sac. Down past the **Estellagem Monte Verde**, we emerge onto the **Caminho da Casa Branca** where we go right to stroll down past the tourist bar/restaurants to the **Hotel Monumental Lido** (Wp.46 136M).

From the tranquil surroundings of **Monte** our second route is truly 'Body & Soul' as we climb up to the historical monument at **Terreiro da Luta**. Our rewards are the impressive 'peace' monument's superb elevated setting with views down over Funchal before returning by country paths. Arriving at **Monte** on the 'roller coaster' bus ride (Funchal Town Bus N°48) from the **Lido** hotel area also adds a new dimension to this exploration of the rural outskirts of **Funchal**.

| 3 | 1½ H | 3 km | 250m / 250m | ↻ | 0 | 2* |

*(in **Monte** square)

Access by car:
Park either at **Monte** (follow the car park signs, park and then follow the walking signs to **Monte** square), or at **Babosas** church square and walk back.

Access by bus:
Take a Funchal Town Bus N° 21, 22 or 48 to **Monte** square.

Starting from the bar in **Monte** square (Wp.1 0M), we take the paths that zigzag up the slope above the square, always choosing the uphill paths at junctions, to come onto the **Vereda da Monte**, a narrow road above the gardens, at a junction (Wp.2 4M).

A narrow lane opposite us drops onto the road (our return route), as we go left on the narrow road, passing a station of the **Calvario** route.

On the zigzag paths

Our road narrows to a *caminho rural* as it winds round amongst the higher houses of **Monte**, steadily climbing up to the right. This steady ascent takes us past stations 2, 3, 4 and 5 of the **Calvario** before coming up to a junction by new houses (Wp.3 15M). At the junction, a cobbled trail goes downhill to the right (our return route) while we take a wide cobbled trail to the left to begin climbing up past new houses on our right. A narrow rushing *levada* keeps us company, then we come into forested slopes.

A steady climb on the well-made trail - almost a 'puff and grunt' ascent - takes us past the sixth station of the cross (Wp.4). Dirt roads have been cut into the slopes on the left of our route, as we pass a walking trail off to the right (Wp.5), before reaching the seventh station of the cross (Wp.6 22M). The urgently rushing *levada* is always with us as we continue climbing on the wide cobbled trail, the water channel tunnelled under our route as we ascend through sharp bends.

The crosses provide convenient excuses for breaks in our relentless ascent up through these steep, forested slopes; we pass the eighth (Wp.7), ninth (Wp.8), tenth (Wp.9), eleventh (Wp.10) and twelfth stations (Wp.11) before coming to the **Spring of the Shepherdess**, where in 1495, the 'Lady of Monte' appeared (Wp.12 35M).

The steepness of our cobbled trail is partly disguised by its green nature, as we climb up past stations thirteen (Wp.13) and fourteen (Wp.14) before reaching walled gardens and a junction with a cobbled path off to our right.

Taking the cobbled path, we have a short climb to reach a 'flat' tarmac road (Wp.15), although you could continue up the wider trail to emerge at the **Monte** road junction and 'dog-leg' back.

The 14th Station of the Cross

Our Lady of Peace statue

Now it's a gentle stroll along the comforting tarmac (watching out for traffic) to the travellers' spring (Wp.16 44M), now somewhat battered and worse for wear. Wide stone steps lead us up to the statue of **Our Lady Of Peace** with its massive chain railings, at one of the best *miradouro* viewpoints overlooking **Funchal**.

After that 250 metre ascent, it is pure pleasure to rest while enjoying the views from this surprisingly little-visited monument. The chains date back to the shelling of **Funchal** harbour in World War 1, after which the chains were hauled by hand up the steep slopes to the **Terreiro da Luta** monument.

We return from the monument by our outward route, the steep nature of the cobbled trail now clearly noticeable on our descent, continuing until we reach the narrow tarmac lane (Wp.3). Here we go straight over onto the cobbled path with the *levada* rushing beside it. Our route descends past rural houses and cultivated plots, with walkways accessing the houses (Wps.17&18). Route finding is easy, but if in doubt, simply follow the *levada* downhill past the walkway of **Vereda dos Quintos** (Wp.19) and onto a steeper section.

Zigzagging down past house N°11, we drop down between walls to come to the end of **Camino das Lajinhas** (Wp.2) and meet our outward route. A simple stroll down the paths from **Vereda da Fonte** brings us back to bar level, and some well-earned refreshment (90M).

Meeting Wp.3 at Caminho das Lajinhas

Beware well-signed walking routes! A couple of clear signs and a manicured start do not always indicate an easy route, as we find on this interesting descent into **Funchal**.

Starting from **Babosas** (or **Monte**, adding ten minutes), we descend the eastern side of the steep valley on a forest path and a little-known *levada* before meeting the **Bom Sucesso** region for a final descent on urban paths to the sea front of **Funchal**. 550 metres of almost continuous descent is tough on the knees even with the best cushioned footwear, though this is a beautiful woodland route along a rarely seen valley, if tougher than its start implies.

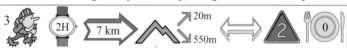

Access by bus or *teleférico*:

	Alternative Start
Arrive at **Babosas** on Funchal Town Bus N° 22, or stroll around from **Monte** (Town Buses 20, 21 & 48). There are two *teleféricos*; N°1 links **Funchal** and **Babosas**.	Bus to Monte and stroll around to **Babosas** square. Add 10 minutes to the main route.

Babosas Church

We start out from **Babosas** church square (Wp.1 0M) with its parking area and bus terminus, taking the cobbled path down into the valley, signed 'Lev. dos Tornos, Lev. Bom Sucesso, Curral Romeiros' - this section of path is common to Walks 3, 4 and 5.

After descending for a few minutes, the **Levada dos Tornos** path (Walk 5) is signed off to our left (Wp.2 12M), while we continue down the right hand trail to cross the stone bridge (Wp.3) before climbing up to a path junction (Wp.4 22M) signed right to 'Levada do Bom Sucesso'.

Turning off the main trail, we drop down the eastern side of the valley on a log-stepped descent, remains of rustic handrails lining the woodland path in places.

A particularly steep zigzag (Wp.5 30M) brings us down to a flat clearing before we continue down through the forest on wooden steps as churning river sounds rise up to us from the rocky watercourse below. Passing evidence of an old wall (Wp.6), we come to a T-junction, where going right will take you to a waterfall, while our onward route (signed 'Levada do Bom Sucesso') is left.

Our path levels out for a section, passing a cave on the left (Wp.7) before descending again alongside the steep gorge with its rushing torrent.

Another steep descent (Wp.8 46M) brings us close to the surging waters, before we cross a rock-filled gully (Wp.9) to contour along the valley wall in gentle descents, the impressive **Via Rápida** bridge dominating the view ahead.

On the steep log-stepped descent

A red and yellow waymark (Wp.10) confirms our route (there is only this route), just before a path junction signed 'Levada dos Tornos & Monte' right, 'Levada Bom Sucesso' left, and 'Curral dos Romeiros' on a path climbing up to our left.

At the next faint path junction (Wp.11) we keep right to descend beside flimsy guard rails before passing log steps which climb up to the left (Wp.12), and then stone steps (Wp.13) and a wire guard rail bring us down to a stone bridge (Wp.14 68M) which marks the start of the **Levada do Bom Sucesso**.

Looking back across the valley, we see that we've walked through the remains of a substantial house and terraces to reach the start of the *levada*. The **Levada do Bom Sucesso** (dry) marks the end of the woodland descent, as we edge round a rock face to walk above sheer drops, before reaching a less vertiginous section (Wp.15) facing the **Via Rápida** bridge (75M). We curve into a small side valley beneath the remains of a substantial house to cross an aqueduct bridge (Wp.16) where a missing slab at its midpoint needs careful footwork.

Coming out of the valley, we are hit by traffic noise as we stroll along to pass under the **Via Rápida** (Wp.17 87M), our path running below the *levada* for a short section before coming back onto its wall and the first houses of **Bom Sucesso** come into view.

Past the first houses, we come to the end of a tarmac road (Wp.18) to take a pedestrian stairway down to our right. Down between tight-packed houses, we reach a tarmac road (Wp.19 102M); crossing carefully, we go onto the **João Gomez** walkway to continue dropping down through the houses, passing walkways off to our left. More walkways branch off the main route as we continue steeply down to emerge from the **Travesa de Ribeira João Gomez** onto the pavement by the main road (Wp.20 107M). Turning downhill, we stroll down pavements and across a tiny square, the road becoming fully commercialised before we reach our finish at the taxi rank (Wp.21 121M) just before the sea front in **Funchal**.

Historic health resort, ornamental gardens, sledge run, cable car, cobbled roads and old stone-laid walking trails threading their way through beautiful countryside, make this one of our short route favourites. A steep drop into the valley and an equally steep climb up the far side is a small price to pay for such beauty.

For Walk! Madeira we walk this delightful cobbled path - quite the best example of traditional Madeiran cobbled trail on the island - from **Romeiros** to **Monte**. In the opposite direction the path junction priorities direct walkers onto **Levada dos Tornos** (Walk 5, 'New Levada dos Tornos: Babosas/Monte - Curral Romeiros'), which means this classic path is now little walked; and as the new bus terminus at **Romeiros** is directly on the start of the path, navigation could not be easier.

A further benefit of starting from **Romeiros** is that our climb out of the **João Gomez** river valley is rewarded by arriving at a spectacularly situated café terrace; quite the best reason for this approach!

* **Babosas** & **Monte**

Access by bus:
Taking Town Bus N°29, we ride up through the suburbs of **Funchal** and after **Bar Miranda** travel below the route of Walk 6, 'Tea & Scones: Romeiros - Jasmin Tea House', before arriving at **Romeiros**, where they've extended the road so we stay seated until we reach the new terminus at the edge of **Romeiros**.

Alighting from the bus (Wp.1 0M), we follow a narrow street (W) to the end of the houses where we find the traditional cobbled path in immaculate condition, to contour along with views over the steep **João Gomez** valley to **Babosas**.

Leaving Curral Romeiros on the cobbled path

Our cobbled path starts its steady descent down the eastern valley wall amongst mimosa and eucalyptus trees, a 'stone rippled' steep zig-zag section dropping us down to a junction (Wp.2 15M) where Walk 3 'Bom Successo; The Route To Town' route drops into the trees on our left (signed).

Continuing down, the gradient then moderates before taking us out onto an impressive stone bridge (Wp.3 21M).

The impressive stone bridge

From above the tumbling waters of the **Ribeira João Gomez** there's only one way and it's upwards, our cobbled trail steadily ascending the wooded western slopes.

Emerging from the trees, we come up to the **Levada dos Tornos** path junction (Wp.4 26M; Walk 5, 'New Levada dos Tornos - Monte/Babosas - Curral Romeiros'); now you can see why our path is so quiet, as the signs give priority to the *levada* route.

Wild flowers en route

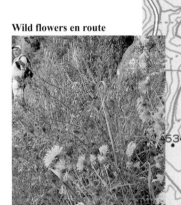

Still climbing, we come up to the **Botánico Teleférico** terminal, giving us another chance to catch our breath, before a final steep slog brings us up to the square in front of **Babosas** church and a wonderfully sited cafe (Wp.5 39M) - actually the back of, and an afterthought of the **Botánico Teleférico** office but still the best sited

The *teleférico* at **Babosas**

refreshment stop overlooking the valley from its small terrace.

Leaving the café, all the climbing is behind us as we stroll across the square to pass the **Funchal-Monte Teléferico** (Wp.6 42M) and the **Monte Palace Gardens** entrance before coming to the top of the **Monte Sled Run** (Wp.7 46M) where we curve right on the broad cobbled path to arrive in the square at **Monte** (Wp.8 45M).

Shrine in Monte square

5 'NEW' LEVADA DOS TORNOS: MONTE/BABOSAS - CURRAL ROMEIROS

Compared to the traditional walking route between **Monte/Babosas** and **Curral Romeiros**, this longer route offers more excitement in the form of an impressive waterfall and a superbly constructed *levada*, but it comes at the price of a vertigo risk; luckily not as high as when we first walked this route as the previously flimsy, or non-existent, protective rails have been substantially upgraded.

A well-signed start and a straightforward ascent to the water channel is followed by long sections of railed *levada* wall above sheer drops; spectacular but could unnerve vertigo sufferers. If in doubt, turn back at the waterfall and take Walk 4 in reverse. Should you start to suffer from vertigo while traversing the sheer eastern wall of the valley, the safest option is to climb down into the *levada*; unusual as this sounds, this option makes for easy walking in cool water, with the protection of the *levada* wall - though the new railings should make this unusual approach unnecessary.

Access by Bus:
Town Buses Nºs 20, 21 & 48, or the *teléferico* for a spectacular ascent from **Funchal** seafront.

Signs at Babosas square

Starting out from the square at **Monte** (Wp.1 0M), we take the level cobbled road to curve round the gardens below the church, passing the sleds and the *teléferico* Nº1 cable car station, before strolling across **Babosas** church square to the cafe at the start a signed walking route (Wp.2 7M).

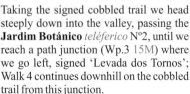

Taking the signed cobbled trail we head steeply down into the valley, passing the **Jardim Botánico** *teléferico* Nº2, until we reach a path junction (Wp.3 15M) where we go left, signed 'Levada dos Tornos'; Walk 4 continues downhill on the cobbled trail from this junction.

The sign at Wp.3

Our dirt path contours along the valley wall until we swing left (17M) up the line of the valley. It is gently uphill, getting steeper between cliffs and the plunging valley, our relentless ascent alleviated by beautiful flora attended by clouds of butterflies.

We come up to a fallen tree (27M) which provides a comfortable rest point, before our final ascent to meet the **Levada dos Tornos** (Wp.4 31M) where it emerges from its long tunnel through the mountains.

The impressive waterfall (Wp.5)

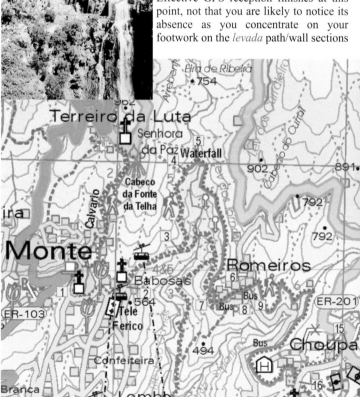

Going right, we follow the *levada* round to its tunnel (Wp.5) beneath an impressive waterfall which plunges to the river bed below.

Effective GPS reception finishes at this point, not that you are likely to notice its absence as you concentrate on your footwork on the *levada* path/wall sections ahead. Careful footwork in the tunnel, then we emerge to different scenery, the wooded western slopes replaced by sheer cliffs. Now it is careful footwork all the way on the *levada* wall, passing a spring in this orogenical landscape, before coming to the best viewing point for the waterfall.

The **Levada dos Tornos** traverses the eastern cliffs, and most of this section would be highly vertiginous but for the new safety railings; if you are suffering on this section, don't forget our advice; walk in the water channel itself. On a hot day, the twenty centimetre deep water is pleasantly cooling, and the side of the *levada* reassuringly safe.

Eventually the sheer drops are behind us, as we pass a cobbled path down to our right, after which we enjoy superb views out over **Funchal** before coming under the first houses of **Romeiros**. Walkways run off the path; at a T-junction, we go right and left to meet the *levada* again at the top of a flight of steps where a downhill path leads to the **Romeiros** bus stop and parking area. Further along the *levada* is the second path which comes up from the bus stop, and starts our route to the **Jasmin Tea House** on Walk 6.

Running along the 600-metre contour, the **Levada dos Tornos** forms part of south-east Madeira's water system and its broad *levada* path makes it a popular walking route. This section is close to **Funchal** with easy access by bus and easy strolling while providing a mixture of old and new woodland, country houses and a notable refreshment stop at the **Jasmin Tea House**. This route is also a logical extension of Walk 4 (in reverse) and Walk 5.

Access by bus:
Take the **Funchal** Town Bus N°29 to **Romeiros**. .

We arrive at the 'Monk's Refuge' village of **Romeiros** on the N°29 bus, or after completing Walk 4 (in reverse) or 5. If you are walking this route in wet weather, you should ask the driver for **Levada dos Tornos** and climb the concrete stair from the bus stop up to join the water channel to join the main route at Wp.2, approximately 1km and 22 minutes from the first bus stop at **Romeiros**, you will then have avoided the old forest section along with its water runoffs, which become slippery and hazardous when water is running.

From the first **Romeiros** bus stop, we take the concrete steps and cobbled path which goes steeply up towards the village. Where the path levels out we go up

concrete steps on the right to come up to the *levada* beside a pale blue 'country station' style building (Wp.1 0M).

Leaving the village behind

Turning right, we leave the village behind to stroll along the broad *levada* path lined with a profusion of wild flowers. Almost immediately (4M) we need to negotiate a watercourse before coming back onto the *levada* path.

The colourful countryside setting changes as we follow the water channel into a steep pocket of the valley wall, the old dark forest enveloping us as cross the steep ravine's black rock water runoff. Out of the pocket, we turn into a second pocket of old forest, crossing another water runoff set in a dark green environment.

The levada at Wp.2

Emerging from this pocket, the old forest gives way to tall eucalyptus trees which give our route an airy feel as we stroll along above the **Romeiros** road with views down the valley. Passing caves in the cliff on our left, we come to a section where the *levada* has been straightened and broad steps cross it (Wp.2 22M) above a bus stop on the road below us; this is the alternative start point in wet weather.

Curving left, this idyllic path is rudely interrupted by the gate (Wp.3) at **Choupana Hills Resort**; the owners of this hotel wanted to close the path, but public pressure has kept this 'public right of way' open.

Through the gate, keep to the *levada* path to pass between the seldom-occupied hotel units, and leaving the accommodation behind (Wp.4), we walk below a large wall before coming to a green gate (Wp.5) at the start of **Choupana** proper above a duck pond and vegetable plots.

Past a house whose terrace forms the *levada* wall, the channel disappears into a tunnel as we come up onto a tarmac lane (Wp.6 30M); Walk 8 comes down this lane on its way down to **Bar Miranda**.

Looking back from Wp.6

Across the lane, we go through a red metal door, signed 'Levada dos Tornos, Levada to Camacha', to enter the grounds of **Quinta do Pomar**. As we come towards the house, we have the choice of negotiating a very narrow *levada* wall, or of following a footpath up through agapanthus above the channel. The cobbled path comes back down to the water channel by a wood shed, then we continue our stroll along to a large water change point alongside a substantial circular water tank (Wp.7 34M), shortly before crossing a steep tarmac lane (Wp.8). Our path passes a patch of houses (Wp.9 42M) which contrast with the meadow landscape and views over **Funchal**, water runoffs bridged over the *levada* before we pass below a house, followed by a road which is bridged over the water channel (Wp.10 49M); a N°47 bus stop sits on the road above our route.

Another couple of minutes along the agapanthus-lined route takes us over a concrete lane by the entrance to **Hortensa Gardens**, a large circular water tank on our right as we stroll along to pass a particularly ugly pig farm (Wp.11), just one small blot on this beautiful route. Passing small abandoned buildings, several trails running off the *levada* path in this region, traffic noise is likely to give an early warning of our arrival at the E-201 road (Wp.12 60M).

Across the E-201, the trees lining the *levada* path have been cleared which results in a potentially vertiginous section of the route requiring careful footwork. If you find this section of path unsettling then head down the road to the **Jasmin Tea House** driveway entrance, approximately 600 metres downhill followed by a steep climb up the driveway.

We follow the *levada* path, we carefully traverse the bare section of path directly above the road (approximately 80 metres), before returning to gentle woodland strolling until we arrive at the *levada* entrance to the **Jasmin Tea House** (Wp.13).

The log steps down to the Jasmin Tea House

Down the log steps, we drop into the tea house terrace (64M) for a selection of home-made refreshments and a vast range of teas served in a delightful setting. While relaxing at the **Jasmin Tea House** we can contemplate onwards routes (perhaps Walk 7), or we have the choice of returning to **Funchal** on the N°47 bus which stops at the bottom of its driveway.

Levada dos Tornos provides easy walking through beautiful countryside. This section of the *levada* offers extensive views combined with rural settlements, before a landslide curtails our progress by *levada* at **Noguiera**. Originally our final section followed the road uphill to **Camacha Shopping** (whose air conditioning provides a cool refuge on hot days), but now we have extended our route to take in another section of *levada* before making a steep tarmac climb up to the square in **Camacha**.

Halfway through our route we encounter a tunnel (ten minutes of narrow messy edging along with a good torch) where we offer an 'over ground' route option to rejoin the *levada* later on for our final section into **Camacha**.

*At **Jasmin Tea House** or **Camacha**

Access by Bus: Town Bus N°47 to Jasmin Tea House, or as an extension of our Walk 6 route from **Romeiros**. Return by N°77 bus from **Camacha** to **Funchal**.

The start at the Jasmin Tea House

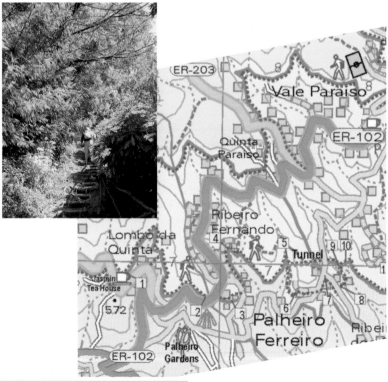

From the **Jasmin Tea House**, we take the steep log-stepped path to climb up onto (or rejoin) the **Levada dos Tornos** (Wp.1 0M) to head west along the waterway. It is an easy stroll along the flower lined canal as it contours round the hillside overlooking the main road settlements.

After crossing the line of a watercourse we pass below houses before meeting the top level of valley housing, and a path climbing up to a white house above the *levada*. Traffic noise increases, mainly heavy lorries grinding their way up the steep road, as we come along to meet the main ER-102 road (Wp.2 17M).

Exercising extreme caution, we cross over the road to come back onto the concrete *levada* path signed 'Levada dos Tornos, Camacha'. **Palheiro Golf** and large *lagos* are away on our right as we wind our way between houses and cultivated plots. As the water channel curves left there is a building on our right with access to its roof just before the *levada* goes underground by a large warehouse (Wp.3 20M). Here, we go left onto a driveway past the warehouse to emerge onto a tarmac road.

Across the road, the flower-bedecked *levada* continues, taking us past houses and a smelly barn before heading into the countryside. Tall eucalyptus trees soar skywards as we swing right at a water runoff below two houses (Wp.4). Fallen trees bridge the water channel, just before we come to a filtration point beside the start of the *levada* tunnel (Wp.5 33M).

Entering the tunnel at Wp.5

Tunnel Route

The tunnel is low, narrow, and gets narrower in the middle; if choosing this route, have a good torch and be careful not to bump your head or let the wall edge you off the narrow, slippery path.

The small window of light at the end of the tunnel seems temptingly close, but it is ten to fifteen minutes of uncomfortable edging along before you reach it.

'Over-Ground' Alternative

Here is our choice for an open air, overland, alternative route.

A steep stepped path takes us up from the tunnel entrance through young trees before levelling off to contour across the slopes before passing a house (Wp.6) beside a concrete road. Down the concrete we reach a tarmac road, where we go left to come up to a junction (Wp.7 16M), with the sign 'Estrada do Pinheirino' on an old building.

Going right past a defunct water tap, we stroll down the tarmac lane to go left at a 'Levada Camacha' sign on a house driveway (Wp.8 19M). A cobbled lane beside the house drops us down past a collapsed hut, to a water tank with a white arrow. Our path splits, both sections heading up the valley before rejoining to cross a plank bridge (Wp.9 25M) and come onto the *levada*. Turning right, we pass a large tree which bridges the water channel (Wp.10); if you are walking this route in reverse, look for this tree as the path off the *levada* one minute later is easily missed.

Fine views after the tunnel

Post-Tunnel official route

Emerging from the tunnel you'll probably take a few minutes cleaning-up and basking in the sunshine before setting off along the *levada* path to pass our 'over-ground' path (Wp.9) and ducking below the fallen tree (Wp.10 35M). We are back to *levada* strolling, passing a broad dirt path off to our right before coming up to cross the **Rua do Pomar** road (Wp.11 44M).

The *levada* and path curve round below affluent houses, to head back into woodland and across a water run-off (Wp.12 49M), and we swing into a new valley with houses across from us; the new **Camacha** 'main' road below us contrasting with our rural landscape.

Lush vegetation after the tunnel

Dead trees bridge the water channel as we stroll past a stream and an impressive stone stair which leads to houses hidden among the trees (Wp.13 54M). **Levada dos Tornos** now runs between houses and workshops, with noisy dogs, where we step up and onto a roadway (Wp.14 57M) curving above the *levada*.

Heading along the road we can look across to where the *levada* is piped across a landslide that dictates this tarmac section of our route.

Our road turns uphill for a steep, slogging ascent past **Pastelaria Can Diro** (67M), a useful if simple refreshment stop on its impoverished terrace to a T-junction (Wp.16) where we go straight over to head through the **Nogueira** housing estate to come onto the ER-205 **Rua da Nogueira** road, opposite a modern factory (Wp.17 69M). Going left we head uphill to take the street right (Wp.18) that runs above the factory.

Alternative Finish at Camacha Shopping.
Originally our route continued up the ER-205, passing the road off to the football pitches before passing under the **Camacha** bypass and slogging up past the **Camacha Shopping** commercial centre; impossible to miss.

Finally coming up to the ER-102 junction, once the main road but now bypassed by the new road we passed under, where there is a pleasant café/*pastelaria* on the junction opposite the bus stop. Other alternatives to catching the bus back to **Funchal** include following our Walk 8 'Levada da Serra' route to **Bar Miranda** (the *levada* is signed from the junction), or **Walk 9 Levada da Serra** to **Camacha**.

Official Finish on Levada dos Tornos
Past the factory we cross over the **Caminho Municipal Dos Caboucos** junction to go down the **Caminho Fonte Concelos** lane passing under the new bridge followed by a small bridge over a watercourse.

Although it looks as if we have lost the *levada*, as we start following the lane uphill we come to an old 'Levada dos Tornos' sign (Wp.19 79M) partially hidden by plant growth. Leaving the lane on the tiny path at a junction we could head straight down to the *levada* or angle through the woods, our choice and keeping right at another path junction we come down to rejoin the water channel (Wp.20 85M). Turning left, we cross a substantial concrete stair before going over an access lane (Wp.21 87M) to return to our *levada* woodland stroll before coming to cross a steep tarmac street (Wp.22 92M).

Over the street, we have a short section of *levada* path running above a steep valley before descending to the road where the *levada* is fenced off at a house. Just along the lane (E) a muddy, log stepped dirt path ascends to the *levada**, signed, though the sign looks most fragile. This path leads up to the next tunnel, so we choose to stay on the lane for a steep ascent up the tarmac to meet the route of Walk 10, 'Levada do Caniço', at **Bar Eira Salgada** (Wp.23 104M).

Turning left, we now have an achingly steep creep up the small lane, our gradient easing slightly at a new junction where we meet our 'Tunnel Finish'.

More steep slogging up the tarmac takes us onto the bridge over the **Camacha** bypass from where it's a comparatively relaxed stroll up to the square in **Camacha** (Wp.24 120M).

Views from the steep lane

* Tunnel Finish

Tunnel aficionados should take the tunnel through to the next valley; in practice a spectacular gorge, to continue on the *levada* path. When you see the supporting wall of a new road ahead leave the *levada* by a traditional cottage to take the steps with green railings up to the cul-de-sac end of a lane. A steady ascent up the lane, getting steeper, will then bring you up to join our official route.

Levada da Serra is southern Madeira's walking motorway, its broad, vertigo-free path allowing relaxed walking through beautiful countryside - only a lack of running water in the *levada* is missing from this near-perfect equation. After the initial climb up from the **Camacha Shopping** junction, it is easy strolling through woodland and an abundance of wild flowers, before finishing on the steep road down through **Choupana**, to the N°30 bus terminus at **Bar/Restaurant Miranda**.

Access by bus:
Camacha Shopping is a convenient start/finish point for walks as it offers frequent bus access and refreshments, unlike the ER-203 drop off point favoured by guided walk providers on the **Levada da Serra**. This is a linear route with easy access on N°29 **Camacha** and N°77 **Santo da Serra** bus routes.

Camacha Shopping junction is our jumping-off point, succumbing to the temptations of the café before tackling either the west and east tours on the **Levada da Serra**. From the junction (Wp.1 0M), the *levada* is signed up a tarmac road. It's a slogging ascent - funny how a climb up a tarmac road is more burdensome than on a walking trail - up past the distraction of a volcanic 'bomb' embedded in the earth wall on our right, then new buildings (Wp.2 5M) before we reach a junction with **Caminho dos Namorados** (Wp.3 12M) where the **Levada da Serra** crosses under the **Caminho da Madeira**, the road continuing up to service a football ground.

The volcanic 'bomb'

Turning left, we are rewarded with relaxed woodland strolling alongside the agapanthus-lined water channel. In this idyllic setting, it is a surprise to find ourselves swinging right to face a huge concrete wall (Wp.4 17M) which supports the football ground, but this incongruity is soon passed for us to return to agapanthus beside the tree-lined path with lush swathes of wild gladioli cloaking the slopes.

Our stroll continues through a pocket in the valley wall (Wp.5 23M) complete with tinkling spring, before passing below a

... relaxed woodland strolling ...

house and then crossing the **Caminho Ribeira Grande** (Wp.6 27M) below **Quinta Proteas**.

Leaving the narrow road behind, we cross a stream on a stone bridge (Wp.7 30M), followed by a second stream and a path up to the right before passing below houses serviced by concrete steps. The **Casa do Til** chalets below the *levada* herald our arrival at the ER-203 road (Wp.8 35M) the dropping off point for coach loads of walkers who will be guided eastwards to **Camacha**.

Across the road, our car-width path accesses garages and then narrows to a broad walking trail which crosses the cobbled access road to **Quinta Vale Paraiso** (Wp.9 40M), with the main road away down on our left. Now we are back into woodland and flowers, a cobbled path crossing our route before we stroll through soaring eucalyptus and pines to pass a picturesque waterfall (Wp.10 48M).

… great drifts of flowers …

The *levada* runs into a small tunnel (Wp.11 52M) where our path rises to cross a cobbled road, before dropping back down alongside the water channel.

Our easy stroll continues over a watercourse, great drifts of flowers covering the hillsides along this section, before bringing us to the ruin of a hut (Wp.12 61M) where what little water there is in the *levada* is diverted into a downhill channel.

The *levada* may be virtually dry, but this only helps to make the route even more floriferous, with plants packing the earth

floriferous, with plants packing the earth channel. In these beautiful surroundings it is easy to miss the point where the channel disappears, before paths cross our route (Wp.13 72M); keep to the main path, and in another couple of minutes, we come to a steep cobbled lane (Wp.14 74M).

After more than an hour of gradient-free strolling, we now skitter down the cobbled lane to cross the ER-201 road (Wp.15 80M), with the football stadium on our left; basic refreshments are available in the stadium's small bar, if open. We follow the lane down past the first houses to pass the road to the **Choupana Hills Resort**, and cross the route of Walk 6 (Wp.16 91M).

Below the **Quinta do Pomar**, we continue down the steep lane past houses on our right until the tarmac lane swings left (Wp.17 98M). We continue straight ahead down a steep street with a stepped pavement, becoming even steeper before it drops us onto the road opposite **Bar/Rest Miranda** (Wp.18 103M).

On our right is the N°30 bus terminus and the **Romeiros** road; the N°29 bus also passes here. If the bus schedule allows, reward yourself in **Bar Miranda** with its *tipico* menu and *miradouro* views over **Funchal**.

Bar Miranda

Levada da Serra East to **Camach**a is southern Madeira's walking motorway, its broad, vertigo-free path making it popular with guided strollers; who usually start 40 minutes away at the ER-203. After the initial climb up from the **Camacha Shopping** junction, it is easy strolling through woodland, wild flowers and traditional settlements. There is even a refreshment stop, **Bar Moises**, half an hour in.. We've extended our original version of this route in our '35 Madeira Walks' to take in the valley to **Rochao** with a finish on the ER-102 and a little-known *levada* before dropping down into **Camacha**.

Camacha Shopping is a convenient start/finish point for walks with frequent bus access and refreshments; unlike the ER-203 drop off point favoured by guided walks on the **Levada da Serra**.

2 | 1½-2H | 6.5 km | 90m / 120m | 1 | 3

Bus Access:
Linear route with easy access on N°29 **Camacha** and N°77 **Santo da Serra** routes.

Ccircular walk options (for car drivers)
Drivers can park at **Camacha Shopping** and then walk back up the old road from the centre of **Camacha**, (10-15 minutes gently uphill), to make the route circular, or take Walk 7 in reverse to **Noguiera** and then up the ER-205, to make the route circular.

Signs at the start of the slogging ascent

Our start is a repeat of Walk 8; from the **Camacha Shopping** junction (Wp.1 0M) we follow the football and *levada* signs for a slogging ascent up the new road.

We pass beneath what might be a 'volcanic bomb' (Wp.2, see the photo at the start of Walk 8, 'Camacha Shopping - Levada da Serra West - Bar Miranda') set in the bank above us; we're no geologists but it's certainly an interesting 'tear drop' shaped large rock.

More slog takes us to a right hand bend, break to look at the sea, then uphill again to curve left up to the **Caminho dos**

The junction at Wp.3

… amongst old oak trees …

Namorados junction (Wp.3 14M), where the **Levada da Serra** crosses under the **Caminho da Madeira**.

Turning right, we walk beneath old oak trees and stands of eucalyptus as the *levada* swings left into a valley. Houses stand above the water channel with gates opening onto our path, as we tour the valley before crossing a flower-lined concrete path to turn into a smaller pocket in the hillside.

A giant fallen tree en route

Out of this second pocket, we're back amongst oaks with yellow broom lining our route as we stroll along below more houses, concrete stairs

Walk! Madeira 53

running down to the village below as we curve left into a landscape of mixed woodland and wild flowers.

More oak trees accompany our path before the woodland gives way to grass-covered slopes dotted with pines. Across the head of the valley, by a spring, we come back amongst woodland as we move out of the valley.

Turning left into the next valley, a village faces us as we stroll beneath ancient trees, our *levada* path lined with giant specimens of fennel, to the head of the valley which is filled with a vista of endemic plants stretching up the slopes.

Achadina

We swing right towards the village of **Achadina**, our path meandering between village houses before widening out to a concrete lane and steps take us down onto a tarmac lane, the *levada* now channelled alongside the road at head height.

Going left, we walk up the tarmac, the *levada* disappearing underground shortly before we reach **Bar Moises** (Wp.4 35M) beside a cross-roads. Being on a relaxed strolling route we should not pass by the opportunity of relaxed refreshments at this village *tipico*, enlarged since we first walked this route and popular with guided walking groups.

After **Bar Moises** we continue in the same direction over the cross-roads, our route marked as a 'no through road', to meet the water channel again. The road narrows to a concrete track until we leave the village behind to stroll along the broad dirt path beneath old oaks, then swing left round a red house into a woodland setting.

We get glimpses of a village ahead through ranks of eucalyptus and slender pines, the views getting clearer as we swing out of the trees. Houses with colourful gardens stand above the *levada* as we come into a small valley. Passing an access stair, we come to the head of the valley (Wp.5 46M), where the *levada* runs through a short tunnel. Heading away from the tunnel, yellow broom lines the path before we come into the village of **Igreja** alongside a black boulder wall.

As we pass two garages our path widens to vehicle width and we to come to the **Caminho Municipal de Portela** (Wp.6 48M) crossing the *levada*. Once this tarmac lane was a traditional Madeiran cobbled track running down into **Camacha** and our finish route, but now it is often busier than the ER-102 main road; for a short finish, follow the road downhill and we'll meet you there a little later.

Carefully crossing the new road, we follow the *levada* path into the picturesque **Rochao Valley**, at the head of which the water channel is bridged over a stream (Wp.7 56M) before we head out of the valley towards the settlement of **Rochao**. As we come to the main housing our path widens to a track and then a road, the *levada* disappearing underground as we walk up to a road with a bus stop (Wp.8 64M).

Turning right, we head down the road to come to the ER-102 'main' road (Wp.9 69M); before Madeira's new road system opened we wouldn't have dreamed of walking along the ER-102 but even though it remains classified as a 'main' road, its traffic flow has become more like that of a country lane.

For our finish we turn right to stroll along the ER-102, watching out for the light traffic, passing wicker workshops, **Rochao Bar** and the **Vereda** stairway (Wp.10) which links to the road running down from Wp.6. On the right of the road we come to a paved floriferous *levada* (Wp.11) which takes us above the dropping road and **Bar Goncalves** before crossing a three metre vertiginous section of the path.

We come along behind houses to concrete steps which takes us up onto the road (Wp.12) running down from Wp.6.

Now it is downhill, the road narrowing as it enters **Camacha**, keeping right at a T-junction (Wp.13) to the church and its square. Passing bar/restaurants, we drop down to the main square and the bus stop (Wp.14 98M), where we will catch the N°77 bus back to **Funchal**.

Camacha Church

One of Madeira's most enjoyable routes, **Levada do Caniço** combines a grand canyon and rural settlements with easy route finding, while having only a medium vertigo risk on some sections of the *levada*. Take your time so as to enjoy the spectacular views down the **Porto Novo** valley, before descending on country roads and paths to finish at the **Jardim do Assomada Snack Bar**. It is a route of three distinct parts; a steep descent to the water channel (tough on the knees), a ribbon of a *levada* contouring through a beautiful landscape (careful footwork needed in places), and finally a road descent (those knees again) to **Assomada**.

Not recommended in wet weather, when the steep cobbled path down through **Salgados** can be very slippery. You can walk the route in reverse, but the ascent up tarmac is tiresome.

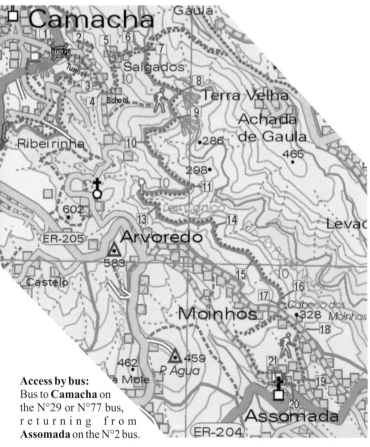

Access by bus:
Bus to **Camacha** on the N°29 or N°77 bus, returning from **Assomada** on the N°2 bus.

Access by car:
Car drivers should park in **Camacha** and taxi back to the start.

The chapel near the route's start

We start out from the **Relogio Café** with its clock tower and shop (0M), famous amongst other things for its long queues for the ladies' toilet, to stroll round the square past the *miradouro* viewpoint, chapel and **Centro de Saúde**, after which we turn right on **Caminho dos Salgados**, signed to 'Veredas, Levada dos Tornos, Assomada, Caniço, Gaula'.

It's steadily downhill, crossing the **Camacha** bypass (Wp.1 3M) before a junction with a broad road which goes left (Wp.2), while our lane swings right, going steeply down before it passes the **Eira Salgada** bar (Wp.3).

The cobbled trail after Wp.4

At a junction in front of a school (Wp.4 10M) we go left, dropping down the cobbled trail past a pink house and descending through tree-shaded slopes. After a zigzag, we skitter down past a pair of houses for the hamlet of **Salgados** to come into view. Concrete steps go down to the right (Wp.5 20M), while we stay on the cobbled trail, passing a concrete path off to houses on our left (Wp.6).

We continue steeply down through this picturesque, flower bedecked hamlet to where red earth replaces the cobbles; our path is clear, but water erosion below the houses has swept away the stone surface, making for a slow, steep descent on a mixture of rock and dirt before we come onto the *levada* (Wp.7 46M).

Porto Novo valley

Looking up the steep sides of the **Porto Novo** valley illustrates how our two hundred metre descent has transported us through a dramatic change in landscape; we've exchanged the urbanisation of **Camacha** for the depths of this wild gorge.

Going right (S), signed to 'Assomada', we stroll along beneath abandoned terraces to pass a green tunnel formed by brambles.

Our route passes through untouched countryside as we pick our way along the narrow *levada* path to pass opposite sheer basalt cliffs, then coming to *miradouro* views down the valley as the canal swings right (Wp.8). We enjoy more views as the canal swings right again (Wp.9 56M) to bring us among gentler, pine-dotted slopes, the *levada* now running in a cutting beside the path.

As we curve into a pocket in the valley wall, the slopes return to near-vertiginous angles, though the drop is shielded by trees and shrubs as we come out of the pocket to pass a hut (Wp.10 65M) before swinging right into the main valley. Here, we meet cultivated terraces which run up the hillside, then swing into another pocket at a *miradouro* viewpoint (Wp.11 70M), and pass stairs to elevated terraces and a spring (Wp.12). Pines dot the slopes, and as we come deeper into the pocket, we cross a slightly vertiginous aqueduct and a waterfall which feeds the *levada* at the apex of the pocket (80M) - a most pleasant spot to take a break.

Coming out of the pocket into the main valley at a *miradouro* viewpoint (Wp.13 85M), our path runs through tree-covered slopes, shady but cutting out the views. One section has suffered landslip damage, before we pass extensive caves (Wp.14). Just past the caves the *levada* drops, foaming, into a broad, tall tunnel, fifty metres long - a luxury tunnel by Madeiran standards - and beyond the tunnel, the rugged nature of our route changes to a broad woodland path.

The Vereda Levada dos Moinhos after Wp.17

The *levada* flows into a deep channel alongside the path (Wp.15 100M), the two coming together again before we reach views over the **Via Rápida** to the small harbour of **Porto Novo**.

Our route comes above cultivated plots before passing broad concrete steps (Wp.16 105M) where the dirt path is replaced by concrete lined with street lights. The **Levada do Caniço** is diverted downhill at the first house (Wp.17 107M), and we follow its route on a ridged concrete path which runs out to the tarmac road at a 'Vereda Levada dos Moinhos' sign.

Below us in the valley is the church of **Assomada**, our destination. We head down the road, passing **Vivenda em Selastina** on our right. After passing **Bar O'Moinho** (closed during our research) the tarmac gets steeper, and we drop down to go left onto **Caminho Quinta dos Roiros** (Wp.18 111M), continuing steeply downhill past houses.

Before meeting the main road, we go right onto **Vereda Quinta dos Louros** (Wp.19 116M) beside impressive *quinta* entrance gates. Our route soon narrows to a path at house N°5, twisting between houses and plots before coming over open ground and up to a street (Wp.20); the 'Travesa da Pedreira' is signed back along our path. Ahead is the welcoming sight of the **Jardim do Assomada Snack Bar** (Wp.21 120M) facing the church, where after two hours on the trail, we can justify indulging in refreshments before catching a bus on the main road for **Caniço** or **Funchal**.

One of the most spectacular *miradouro* viewpoints on Madeira awaits those who undertake this short stroll from **Ribeiro Frio**. The clear trail is gradient and vertigo free, so there are no excuses for even the least energetic stroller to miss this route. If you can pick a cloudless day, even better.

Access by car: *except at the **Balcões** itself, which has railings
Car drivers can park near the bars, lower down the road near the **Balcões** path, or at the picnic areas at the top end of **Ribeiro Frio**. Although buses Nºs 103 and 138 go to **Ribeiro Frio**, they are few and not conveniently timed for walking excursions, so are not recommended.

Magnificent views from Balcões

From **Ribeiro Frio**'s two bars we walk down the road until it swings left, an information board on the corner marking the start of our broad *levada* path (Wp.1 0M). Shaded by mature trees, the road dropping away below us, we stroll through forested slopes, then cross a bridge (Wp.2 5M), passing a large boulder carelessly tossed onto the *levada* before passing through a rock cutting (Wp.3).

Beyond it we look down on houses set above the main road, some with entrances off the *levada* path, reaching the temptingly situated **Bar Flor da Selva** (Wp.4 10M). Oaks line the path as we pass above **Balcões Bar** (shut, possibly permanently) before we come to a channel-side gift shop. The path swings left and we stroll past another pair of rocks, seemingly carelessly tossed onto the *levada* (Wp.5), to arrive at a junction (Wp.6 16M) where 'Balcões' is signed along the right hand path. In wo minutes we're standing on a spectacularly sited viewpoint (Wp.7 18M) protected by rustic railings. Suspended above the landscape, we look down over the **Metade Valley** and the **Fajã da Noguiera** power station, with the high central peaks, front left.

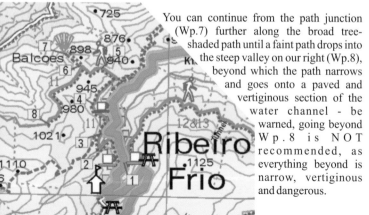

You can continue from the path junction (Wp.7) further along the broad tree-shaded path until a faint path drops into the steep valley on our right (Wp.8), beyond which the path narrows and goes onto a paved and vertiginous section of the water channel - be warned, going beyond Wp.8 is N O T recommended, as everything beyond is narrow, vertiginous and dangerous.

Choosing a favourite Madeiran walking route is difficult, but our **Ribeiro Frio** circular must be in the top ten. Refreshments, parking, the best of **Levada do Furado**, a little-known woodland climb alongside a rushing water channel, a beautiful river setting, an ascent onto the plains and a descent on a cobbled donkey trail - however, definitely not a good choice if wet, so do make this a good weather route only. Another bonus is that the accesses from *levada* and from road are hidden, so you will only meet walkers 'in the know'.

Access by car:
Car drivers can park near **Victor's Bar**, lower down the road near the **Balcões** path (Walk 11), or at the picnic areas at the top end of **Ribeiro Frio**.

Access by bus:
Although N°s 103 and 138 buses go to **Ribeiro Frio**, they are few and not conveniently timed for walking excursions, so are not recommended.

The start of the route at Wp.1

You could start with refreshments in **Victor's Bar** or in the *tipico* opposite. Just below the bar 'PR10 Portela 11km' is signed on a path (Wp.1 0M) taking us over the river bridge and onto the broad *levada* path.

This is a cool, tree-shaded path, smooth underfoot at first - but don't think it's all going to be like this. Soon it becomes lumpy with tree roots and rocks, while the combination of tree cover and steep hillside make for poor GPS reception along much of the **Levada do Furado**.

We progress along this green lane to pass through a rock cutting (Wp.2 15M), crossing a stream's water runoff just before we reach the first of several sections where the *levada* is protected by steel supports and wires (Wp.3). These protected sections are not difficult, but can be annoying if waiting for walkers coming in the opposite direction or when following slow groups of amblers. After this protected section we enjoy our first views over the north coast (Wp.4), followed by a tunnel bored into the hillside, and a stream which feeds the *levada* (Wp.5 20M).

The **Levada do Furado** is a woodland route where tree canopy generally obscures the views, so coming to an open aspect (Wp.6 25M) just before a waterfall provides us with welcome vistas. The guard rails at this point are largely superfluous, though we soon tackle a long section of railed *levada* wall - just hope you don't meet a large walking party coming towards you!

The path opens out after the railed section as we pass through dark laurel forest with a tinkling stream (43M), before reaching a section with rustic handrails protecting us from landslip damage (Wp.7 45M).

As the water channel curves right, the sound of rushing water meets us as we stroll along to a noisy *levada* junction by a bridge over the **Ribeira do Bezerro** (Wp.8 52M). So many walkers take a break at this bridge that the birds expect a snack and will swoop down to beg crumbs, almost perching on your hand.

The noisy *levada* junction (Wp.8)

The 'walking motorway' to **Portela** (Walk 13) carries on over the bridge, but we clamber up to the rushing water channels to follow the higher channel straight uphill. We have a stiff, and wet, climb up through the forest on the narrow path alongside the rushing water channel. Some stone-laid sections of path remain, and log steps help with the ascent as ferns and mosses abound beside our route.

The gradient eases (Wp.9 62M), allowing us to walk rather than climb for a section, before the ascent is rejoined. Leaks and collapsed walls on the rushing water channel mean that much of this path is wet, even in the driest of weather. This is certainly a 'puff and grunt' ascent with plenty of rests, as we progress past a cave (Wp.10 76M) and a spur of rock (Wp.11 81M).

The relentless ascent finally eases as we cross a small stream, and a path goes up to the right (Wp.12 92M); the water channel has branches bridged across it at this point. After a couple of minutes of easy walking, we are negotiating the end of the water channel and the polished rocks of **Ribeiro do Bezerro**

(Wp.13 94M), an idyllic hideaway in which to take a break after that energetic climb.

Refreshed, we set off on the second stage of our tour (0M) by retracing our steps back to the path junction (Wp.12 2M). Turning uphill over the *levada*, we are back to climbing steeply in an almost ladder-like ascent through the trees to reach a crest (Wp.14 6M). After a short drop, we ascend again before clambering over rocky water run-offs (Wp.15 9M), then climb to emerge from the tree heather onto a sloping meadow (Wp.16 15M).

... onto a sloping meadow ...

Suddenly, we find ourselves out in the open; looking around, there is absolutely no sign of human habitation except for a flattened grass trail leading up the meadow past a stone cairn (Wp.17). The slope is more extreme than it first appears as we ascend the path through bracken and tree heather onto a coll (Wp.18 23M).

At last the climb is over as we swing right towards farm buildings, the path confused by goat trails before we come onto a surprising green grass road in front of the farm (28M).

Turning right, we stroll along the grass road, worn areas revealing this to be a broad cobbled road, though why such a well-constructed route should exist in this isolated region is a mystery. As we stroll along the road, it is all too easy to miss the path junction (Wp.19 32M) where we go left on a narrower rippled cobbled path, to descend through a gate. Grass has grown over many of the cobbles as we descend through hairpin bends between tree heathers (Wps.20 & 21) before encountering large rocks beside a spring (Wp.22 45M). Squeezing through the rocks, our cobbled trail continues down to a rather ignominious end where the ER-103 road has obliterated the older route (Wp.23 48M).

The old trail meets tarmac (Wp.23)

We pick our way down onto the tarmac, then head down the road for a couple of minutes before turning off onto a cobbled trail (Wp.24 50M). Once again we're descending through forest, passing dirt roads off to our left before coming alongside the stepped *levada* above the fish farm at **Ribeiro Frio** (Wp.25 60M). A couple of minutes downhill brings us to some well-earned refreshments at the bar of our choice, back at our starting point.

13 PORTELA BOUND

Ribeiro Frio to Portela along the Levada do Furado is one of Madeira's most 'guided' walking routes, despite its being officially rated as 1 star for minimal ascents, and green for 'no danger' (though we disagree), and that it is almost impossible to get lost on route.

Logistically, we suggest driving to Ribeiro Frio in order to enjoy some pre-route refreshments, then walk to Portela (possibly taking in Pico do Suna as an energetic diversion), finishing with refreshments in Portela, then taking a taxi back to Ribeiro Frio. Although this route is officially rated as green for 'no danger', we found plenty of vertiginous sections, and though these are protected by steel posts and wires, they could upset those nervous of heights. Although we give GPS waypoints, reception is poor along much of this route.

*at Ribeiro Frio and Portela

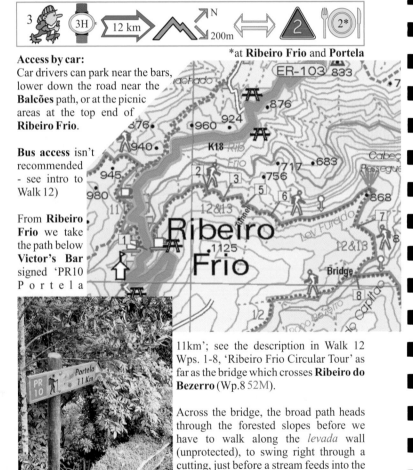

Access by car:
Car drivers can park near the bars, lower down the road near the **Balcões** path, or at the picnic areas at the top end of **Ribeiro Frio**.

Bus access isn't recommended - see intro to Walk 12)

From **Ribeiro Frio** we take the path below **Victor's Bar** signed 'PR10 Portela

The route start at Ribeiro Frio

11km'; see the description in Walk 12 Wps. 1-8, 'Ribeiro Frio Circular Tour' as far as the bridge which crosses **Ribeiro do Bezerro** (Wp.8 52M).

Across the bridge, the broad path heads through the forested slopes before we have to walk along the *levada* wall (unprotected), to swing right through a cutting, just before a stream feeds into the water channel. Our route develops into a pattern of easy *levada* path through forested slopes, mixed with sections of walking along the channel wall, usually protected with steel wires.

The pool, 63 minutes into the route

Now this pattern varies as we temporarily leave the *levada*, firstly to cross a stream below the channel (58M), then dropping below it at a beautiful pool (63M). Our routine is enlivened by a cutting (72M) requiring careful footwork on the slabs over the water channel, followed by second, third and fourth cuttings.

The *levada* goes through an arch (97M) and our path drops down a rock staircase to pass below cliffs and then back up another stair to the water channel, soon dropping down again to cross a stream before rejoining the channel again. The **Levada do Furado** winds through a mixture of dark primeval forest and lighter, airier woodland, but all of it is extremely short of views - that is, until we come to a promontory off the *levada* (112M) where we can walk out for a few metres to enjoy views from **Rocha dos Pingos** down over the north coast. Back on the water channel, we come to a short tunnel (118M) where old paths go left at each end of the tunnel, then climbing over it to give an alternative route up to **Pico do Suna** (Walk 14).

The next excitement is a long vertiginous section (protected by wires) and short tunnels, as the channel curves above the **Cabeço Furado** escarpment. A filtration point on the *levada* (141M) is a welcome sign, as just around the corner we come to the **Lamaceiros Water House** (142M, dated 1906) where the **Levada da Portela** starts its downhill rush.

Lamaceiros Water House

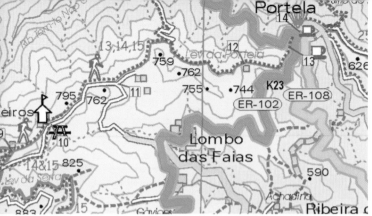

Another couple of minutes along the path, we come to a walking cross-roads (Wp.9 145M); 'Pico do Suna' is signed right, 'Santo da Serra' is straight ahead (5km), 'Ribeiro Frio 8km' and 'Portela' is signed downhill (left).

From the junction (0M) we drop down on a semi-stepped track brings us alongside the small rushing *levada*, to come down to the toilets and forest house at **Lamaceiros** (Wp.10 8M) with its attractive gardens and log-furnished picnic tables. We've come onto a dirt road which we follow downhill to a junction and picnic table (Wp.11 12M) where 'Portela' is signed left.

The log-steps after Wp.12

Going left, we come down to a T-junction (17M), again going left to follow the 'Portela, Porto da Cruz' sign, with the water channel beside us as we pass **Lombo dos Faias** on our right, shortly after which the road runs out. Here, we go right on a path following the *levada*, contouring around the slopes with excellent views out over **Porto da Cruz**.

When we come to the remains of a building on the right (Wp.12 35M), the **Levada da Portela** shoots downhill as we follow it down a log-stepped descent. Our path follows the channel to drop us down

through mature pines and onto the ER-102 road by an information board (Wp.13 44M, 'Ribeiro Frio 12km, 4 hours'). Now it's down the road, noticing the shrine and *miradouro* on the left, to arrive at the taxi rank and the **Miradouro da Portela Bar/Restaurant** (Wp.14 47M, 670 metres altitude).

Lamaceiros Posto Florestal at Wp.14

Madeira has some amazing wizardly towers from which its rangers keep watch for evidence of forest fires. **Pico do Suna**, with its fire watch tower, more Terry Pratchett modern than Harry Potter ethnic, sits on a promontory thrust out from Madeira's northern escarpment. Despite its waymarked and straight forward (if energetic) access, plus spectacular views from a beautiful site, **Pico do Suna** is little visited by walkers. It's their loss, but don't let it be yours - take binoculars and a picnic to fully enjoy the views from the summit.

Access by car:
This is a linear route, up and back, from **Portela**. Park at the **Portela** *miradouro* on the side roads.

Access by bus:
Bus access on N°s 53 or 78 services.

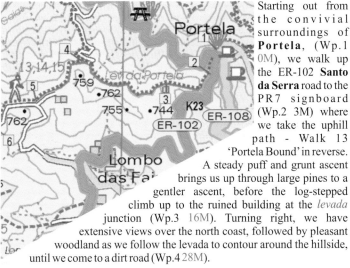

Starting out from the convivial surroundings of **Portela**, (Wp.1 0M), we walk up the ER-102 **Santo da Serra** road to the PR7 signboard (Wp.2 3M) where we take the uphill path - Walk 13 'Portela Bound' in reverse. A steady puff and grunt ascent brings us up through large pines to a gentler ascent, before the log-stepped climb up to the ruined building at the *levada* junction (Wp.3 16M). Turning right, we have extensive views over the north coast, followed by pleasant woodland as we follow the levada to contour around the hillside, until we come to a dirt road (Wp.4 28M).

Lamaceiros Posto Florestal (Wp.7)

On the road, we walk past **Lombo das Faias** to a junction (Wp.5) where we go uphill to a second junction (Wp.6) and again head uphill to arrive at the **Lamaceiros Posto Florestal** (Wp.7 40M). Its log stools and tables, set amongst the garden beds, make this a pleasant spot in which to recover from the climb (so far).

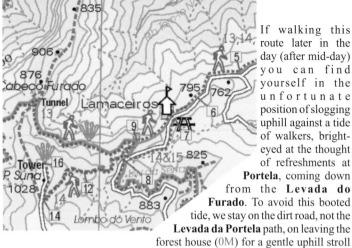

If walking this route later in the day (after mid-day) you can find yourself in the unfortunate position of slogging uphill against a tide of walkers, bright-eyed at the thought of refreshments at **Portela**, coming down from the **Levada do Furado**. To avoid this booted tide, we stay on the dirt road, not the **Levada da Portela** path, on leaving the forest house (0M) for a gentle uphill stroll through the trees. At an old 'Portela' sign nailed to a tree (Wp.8 9M), we go right on a path to join the **Levada da Serra**; this path is easily missed, so if you find yourself crossing the water channel on the dirt road, turn right onto the *levada* path where an easy stroll takes us along to the signed cross-roads (Wp.9 15M) of walking trails.

Pico do Suna is signed left up a grassed-over dirt road. It's a reasonably steep puff-and-grunt ascent up the tree-covered hillside, ducking under a fallen tree (Wp.10 17M) and passing through the remains of a fence (Wp.11 22M), just after a stand of soaring mature pines. It is onwards and upwards, to duck under a second fallen tree (Wp.12 28M), laurel and tree heather beginning to replace the pines as we gain height.

We pass under a fallen tree which bridges the green road (Wp.13 40M), shortly after which we take a footpath which climbs steeply up on our right (Wp.14 43M) to come onto a continuation of the forest track by a spring (Wp.15 45M). (If you miss this path, you can continue up the green road to a junction and go right to find the spring.)

There's still some ascending to do, as we go right to reach the peak (Wp.16 49M, 1047 metres altitude), just before an impressive green fire watch tower. The tree heather in front of the tower has been cut back to form a *miradouro* viewpoint to where the massive bulk of **Águia** (not so massive from our elevated position) towers over **São Roque** and **Porto da Cruz**, a fitting reward for our energetic climb.

We descend by the same route, the steep nature of the green road seeming more extreme now than when we were slogging up it.

The Wizardly Tower, Pico do Suna

The broad paths of **Levada da Serra** have introduced thousands of people to walking in Madeira, though few of them see the western arm beyond **Camacha**. This is an unfortunate omission, as the section above **Lamaceiros** to **Santo da Serra** contains some of the island's best mature woodland, and should be a 'must' for tree aficionados. It is easy walking (1 walker rating) once we've climbed the 180 metres up from **Portela**.

	Extensions for bus users
Access by car: Drivers should park at **Portela** and taxi back from **Santo da Serra**.	If you plan to arrive at **Portela** by bus (N°s 53 or 78), you might consider extending your route along the **Levada da Serra** as far as **Camacha**, to link with our other walks in the area, or make it an 'all day' stroll, in which case, add 3-4 hours to the time allowed, depending upon your walking pace, and 13 kilometres to the distance.

From **Portela** we take the **Levada da Portela** path to climb up to the **Lamaceiros Posto Florestal** forest house (Wps.1-7 40M) (see Walk 14, Pico Do Suna, and Walk 13 Portela Bound, for a detailed description of this section). From the forest house, we stay on the dirt road until it crosses the **Levada da Serra** (Wp.8 50M). Going left on the broad *levada* path, we find ourselves amongst magnificent pines, a particularly prime specimen standing out even in this company of excellent examples (Wp.9 55M).

Minor paths run off up and downhill from the water channel, then we cross a water run-off channelled over the *levada* (Wp.10) just before squeezing round a huge 'hippo-head' boulder. Mature pines block GPS coverage as our path drops down from the channel at a landslip section protected by rustic fencing, then climbs back up to it (65M).

Our stroll brings us through the dappled shade of deep woodland to pass a filtration point on the *levada* (Wp.11), before we reach views of the **Santo da Serra Water House**, illuminated by beams of sunlight (Wp.12 75M). If you've enjoyed the trees so far, you'll love the pines by the water-house.

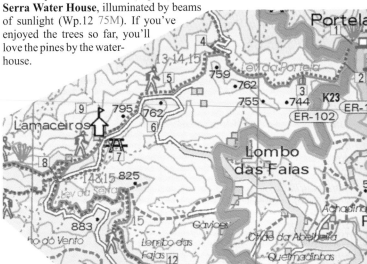

Signs on the water-house show 'Lamaceiros 3km, Portela 5km, Ribeiro Frio 12km' to the west, 'João Ferino 5km, Camacha 15km' signed east, and 'Santo da Serra 2km'. Just past the water-house we go left down a broad track which leaves the woodland behind. Our route comes alongside a dry water channel before it swings right to join another dirt road.

Contorted pines at the Santo da Serra Water House

We leave the track (Wp.13 81M) to follow the paths beside the dry water channel, down through groves of soaring eucalyptus trees. The paths widen into a logging track (Wp.14 85M) which runs down to a chain serving as a vehicle barrier (Wp.15 88M).

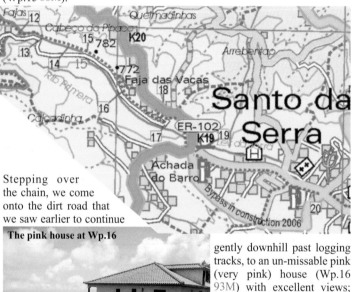

Stepping over the chain, we come onto the dirt road that we saw earlier to continue

The pink house at Wp.16

gently downhill past logging tracks, to an un-missable pink (very pink) house (Wp.16 93M) with excellent views; from here, the road is surfaced.

Now we have an easy stroll down the lane, passing a 'cobbles' workshop (Wp.17) on the left before dropping onto the ER-102 main road (Wp.18 100M). Keeping to the left of the road, we enjoy views over the rich valley before coming down to the **Portela** junction (Wp.19 105M) with the convenient **Casa Bareto** bar for refreshments. The central square of **Santo da Serra** with its taxi rank (Wp.20 115M) is a further ten minutes gentle stroll away through the outskirts of this affluent town.

The **Ribeira de São Roque** valley, a northern version of the **Socorridos** valley, is the spectacular (and highly vertiginous) setting for the source of the **Levada do Castelejo**. Fortunately, once the *levada* turns out of this huge valley, its nature changes and it becomes a quiet blue ribbon which contours around the northern slopes, from above **Cruz** to **Referta**.

Our route passes through this region of rural tranquility; we look down on cultivated plots and small settlements while enjoying excellent flora. Only where a road has recently been constructed off the ER-102 are there any gradients, where stairs take us down to cross the road before climbing up again to the *levada*.

* refreshments are available off the main route

Access by car:
Car drivers should follow the narrow road up from **Cruz**, keeping to the main lane until it crosses the *levada*; there is adequate parking above or below the waterway.

Access by bus:
For access by bus, start at **Referta** and ask for **Levada do Castelejo**; the route takes you to **São Roque** valley and return.

Before the tarmac road ends above **Cruz**, it crosses the **Levada do Castelejo**; we park alongside the tarmac above or below the water channel. The *levada* is signed westwards towards its source, but we go up onto the eastern section (Wp.1 0M) to stroll along the concrete path lined with wild flowers. Other paths cross the channel to access higher plots, before we turn into a small cleft to pass a filtration point (Wp.2 8M), then coming back to northern views as we stroll along and cross a *caminho rural* (Wp.3 12M) with our route clearly signed to 'Referta'. We pass a vine terrace, the vines trained over a framework down the slope below us, and at a house, our path surface changes from concrete to dirt (Wp.4 14M).

Now we enter a wilder environment; mimosas, pines and young oaks become prominent along this section of the water channel. Past concrete constructions (Wp.5 22M), our *levada* is paved and has handrails of electrical flex; we then curve right to pass between a water tank and a concrete road (Wp.6), which serves a house in the next valley.

Fine views from the Levada do Castelejo

Our route curves right into the large valley above **Ribeira Tem-te Não Caias** (which loosely translates as 'Take care not to fall' river), where we pass below an unusual pine with strange leaf growth (Wp.7 30M).

We stroll along the grass, flower-lined path between the tree line above us and the highest cultivated plots below our route - it's a pleasing country route with easy walking, though with few specific features.

A path crosses the *levada* at a *miradouro* viewpoint over the valley (Wp.8 38M), shortly before we come onto a concreted section of the path with

… a *miradouro* viewpoint …

railings as we pass below a house with an access stair down to the road below us. Next, we come to vegetable plots alongside the water channel and a garden hut (Wp.9), as we approach a road which cuts the *levada* path (45M).

A road has been built down the valley from the ER-102, cutting through the water channel; the water is now piped around the valley. We go down the diversion steps to cross the road, climbing up to the continuation of the traditional *levada* (Wp.10). As we pass a house at roof level, the path surface changes to concrete; we stroll along below the new road which contours around the valley wall above us.

Curving right into a wide valley, we come to a section with sturdy handrails (Wp.11 55M) where the water channel has been rebuilt over a landslip, after which we return to relaxed walking, the channel running in and out of clefts in the valley wall where the path is bridged over the water courses. Approaching houses lining a road, we come to a short and relatively comfortable tunnel (65M); you could go over the tunnel on an energetic staired ascent and descent.

Out of the tunnel, the *levada* curves right below houses to come below the bus stop in upper **Referta** where steps take us up onto the 'main' road by the **Cruz da Garda** junction (Wp.12 70M).

There is a shop opposite the bus stop, or you could divert up the **Cruz da Garda** road for *tipico* refreshments as a mini-mercado rural bar, eight minutes walk away (Wp.13). There are bars lower down the ER-102, but it is a slog back uphill to the *levada*.

The **Levada do Castelejo** continues eastwards from the **Cruz da Garda** junction, but the path runs out in under five minutes. We return by our outward route, back to the point where the road crosses the *levada* above **Cruz** (approximately 2½ hours in total).

Extension

Here, we can extend our route by following the 'Lev do Castelejo' sign west past a couple of houses, the broad concrete path changing to narrow dirt at the second house, to where the *levada* turns into the massive **São Roque** valley.

Flowers accompany us en route

From here, the path narrows and cultivated plots cease as the water channel starts to run along the sheer valley walls (7 minutes from the road). The path now has unprotected drops and is highly vertiginous. Only the most experienced mountain walkers with a good head for heights should attempt the path up to the source of the *levada* at **Ribeiro Frio**.

17 THE GREEN POOL
(Caldeirão Verde - nearly)

Take an easy woodland stroll with impressive trees, add in a 'chocolate-box' *pousada*, and a tall waterfall dropping into a green pool, to make one of Madeira's most pleasant easy walks. Adventurous walkers can continue beyond our **Ribeira da Fonte do Louro** finish, on the traditional tunnelled and more vertiginous extension to **Caldeirão Verde**.

2/3 | 2½ H | 8 km | N N | 2 | 3

Access by car:
Take the ER-101 from **Santana**, turning off onto the ER-218 just after the petrol station. There's a the parking area by **Rancho Nadeirense** off the ER-218.

Alternative Short Walk
An easy, vertigo-free stroll; follow the main route to the gravity gate at Wp.10, and return (80 minutes).

Our start point is the parking area by **Rancho Nadeirense** off the ER-218, to take the broad dirt trail (Wp.1 0M) signed 'Levada Walking Quemadas'; **Bar/Rest Nadeirense** is down on our right for refreshments before and/or after the walk.

It's a pleasant woodland stroll beside the water channel, passing an impressive mature pine (Wp.2 3M) just before we come to a path junction where the *levada* goes right. Straight ahead, we meet the channel and path again in a few metres. The *levada* meanders back and forth across the broad, tree-shaded trail, so take care not to step into any of the unpaved holes.

Soaring eucalyptus

Mature pines and eucalyptus soar above us as we pass an old

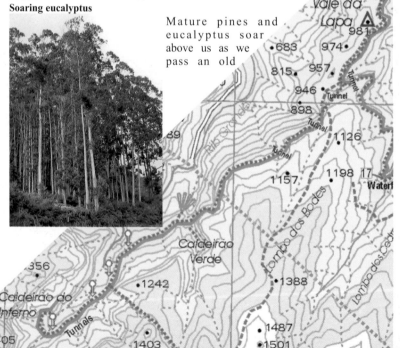

track off to the right (Wp.3 16M) before swinging into a steeper valley where we cross a stone-laid watercourse deep in the forest (Wp.4 20M). We reach a stone-furnished picnic area to cross a rushing stream on a concrete bridge (Wp.5). A plank bridge and guard rails cross a short landslip section before we cross the cobbled *caminho rural* at **Parque dos Quemados** (Wp.6 26M). Caldeirão Verde' and 'Caldeirão Infierno' are signed in front of the picturesque *pousada*, as we stroll across to the duck ponds.

Over a small wooden bridge, we come onto another broad walking trail alongside the *levada*, signed to 'Valle de Lapa, Caldeirão Verde 6.5km, Caldeirão do Infierno 8.5km'. Our route was originally a 'country ride' planted with imported trees, now over a century old, many of these specimen trees still surviving today (Wp.7 30M).

In another couple of minutes, a well-stabilised dirt road crosses the water channel (Wp.8 32M) before we pass an amazing quadruple-trunk pine tree (Wp.9 34M), just before our route narrows as it swings left into a great forested bowl, and we come to a gravity gate (Wp.10 37M).

This gate marks a divide in the route; up to this point it has been a leisurely stroll, but now we alternate between walking on a narrow path and on the *levada* wall, where vertiginous sections benefit from steel uprights and wires. Almost immediately we are edging across one of the wired sections (Wp.11 40M), shortly before the path leaves the water channel to lead us down and across a stream bed (Wp.12 45M), then climbing steeply back up to rejoin the water channel, it having negotiated an impossible wet pocket in the cliff wall.

Now our route curves into the **Ribeira dos Centros** valley where we cross the

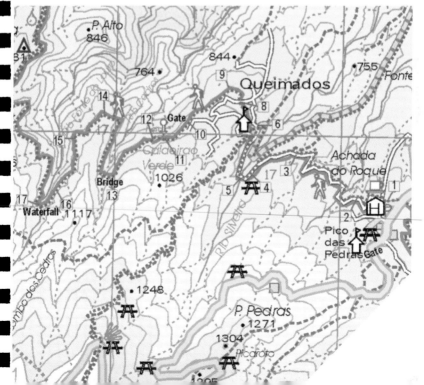

watercourse on a substantial aqueduct bridge (Wp.13 54M). Railed and wire sections predominate, before we come back between trees on each side of the path, more reassuring, though tree heathers cut out the views. Through a small rock cutting (Wp.14 63M), the trees continue until we come into view of the waterfall (Wp.15 67M) which graces our destination at the **Ribeira da Fonte do Louro**.

Concentrating on the path, we come round a corner to a memorable view of the waterfall (Wp.16 75M), just a couple of minutes before we go down to cross the *ribeira* below the pool and its waterfall (Wp.17 77M).

The waterfall at 75 minutes

Don't be surprised to find other walkers taking a break and a picnic in this delightful setting, either at the end of this walk or while recovering from the rigours of **Caldeirão Verde** and **Caldeirão do Infierno**.

At the pool and waterfall

Extension: Caldeirão Verde (Green Cauldron)
The 300 metre high falls of **Caldeirão Verde** are a further hour and four tunnels onward along the *levada*. Fifteen minutes after the fourth tunnel, you reach a water change point, where you take the path up to the left, to see the falls and pool of **Caldeirão Verde**. **Caldeirão do Infierno** is another hour of unprotected drops and tunnels beyond the **Green Cauldron** and is only recommended for experienced walkers with no fear of vertigo.

High peaks are always exhilarating, and **Pico Ruivo** has it all; easy access, simple route finding, spectacularly sited refreshments and even freedom from vertigo - the only Madeiran peak to combine all these features, making this route a must for everyone who can handle the exertion and altitude. Access is by car on the ER-218 road, signed from **Santana**.

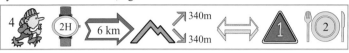

Access by car:

Even reaching the start of this walk is an adventure, once you have found the ER-218 road, just a few metres west of the petrol station at **Santana**. We climb up through cultivated plots and houses, including a couple of small bars, which become less frequent after we pass the football ground and a vehicle wrecker business. Passing **Rancho Nadeirense** (see Walk 17) and the open barrier at **Pico das Pedras Posto Florestal** forest house, we're still only half way to our start point.

Beyond the open barrier the tarmac road is in poorer condition, as we drive up through pines and then tree heather, before coming to views across the high valleys. Eventually, the tarmac ends at a large dirt car park below the abandoned forest house at **Teixeira**. After that motoring ascent of 1300 metres, it's a good idea to take a few minutes acclimatising to the thin air at this altitude before starting out on foot on our ascent.

From the car park (Wp.1 0M), we are soon onto a manicured, stone-laid path which steadily climbs on steps, to give us superb views over the valleys north and south of our broad-backed ridge. A steeper section brings us up to a fence (Wp.2 8M) where our path swings left and then right through the fence, for us to face a long straight incline before coming to the first stone shelter alongside a spring (Wp.3 16M). The only problem on this early section of the route might be swarms of small flies that were magnetically attracted to the yellow and orange shirts we were wearing!

Gentle ascents on the manicured trail bring us to the second stone shelter (Wp.4 23M) and as we cross a gentle crest, the spectacularly sited guest house comes into view a h e a d . Surprisingly, we have a long, steady downhill to a junction (Wp.5 33M) where a narrow dirt path is signed right to **Ilha**.

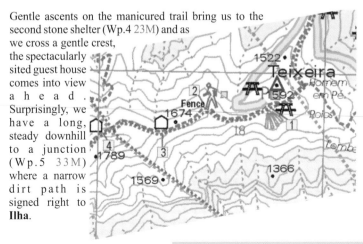

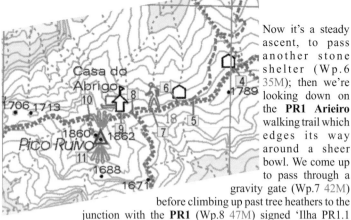

Now it's a steady ascent, to pass another stone shelter (Wp.6 35M); then we're looking down on the **PR1 Arieiro** walking trail which edges its way around a sheer bowl. We come up to pass through a gravity gate (Wp.7 42M) before climbing up past tree heathers to the junction with the **PR1** (Wp.8 47M) signed 'Ilha PR1.1 8.6km, Achada do Teixeira, PR1 Arieiro 6.3km'.

A steep, stepped climb brings us to the guest-house courtyard and a stone shelter (Wp.9 50M), just the place to take a break before the final ascent. In its splendidly isolated location, it's a wonder that the guest-house offers snacks and drinks for sale at all, so be prepared for 'high altitude' prices which are still good value.

Looking back to the guest-house

A cobbled, stepped path starts to ascend from the courtyard and heads towards **Pico Ruivo**. It is a steady, energetic climb to arrive at a path junction below the peak (Wp.10 54M); a sign 'PR1 Encumeada 10.9km, Boca das Torrinhas 5.1km' is a few metres further along the path. Going left, we zigzag up the steep slopes, avoiding the scree shortcuts to arrive breathless on top of **Pico Ruivo** (Wp.11 65M 1862m).

Spectacular views from the peak

Views from the peak are truly spectacular, so it's no surprise that you are likely to be sharing them with plenty of other red-faced, heavy-breathing walkers; the small plateau around the trig point can become quite crowded at times.

The descent back to **Teixeira** is the reverse of our climb, easier physically and accompanied by fine views all the way.

Pico do Ariero

Pico do Arieiro is the most visited peak on Madeira, thanks to easy road access on the ER-202 from the **Poiso** junction. With its large car parking area, a café in the *pousada*, and a well-stocked gewgaw shop, it caters for mass tourism. From the **Arieiro** trig point, just above the *pousada*, there are superb views, but this is just a taster. If you have driven straight up from sea level, we suggest you give yourself a few minutes, perhaps with coffee on the bar terrace, to acclimatise to the thin air at 1800 metres altitude.

From the corner of the *pousada* (Wp.1), a stone-stepped path leads up to the **Arieiro** trig point. At a signboard (Wp.2), the route officially rated as 'orange', a manicured stone slab path heads along the ridge (NW) towards a large knoll. Progress is slowed by the multitude of small steps, as the chasms open up each side of the ridge.

Although the ridge and its path are broad, the beginnings of vertigo are there as we start descending. As we begin the climb to the knoll, guidance posts and wires reassure the unsteady (Wp.3 8M). Coming down the knoll, we descend on more steps, shallow stone steps at first, then larger stone treads as we come to the bottom of the stair (Wp.4 12M). Now we are on a manicured path again with a handrail, though the path is broken away in at least one section. We climb a multitude of shallow steps before passing through a spring-loaded gate, then going right to the first viewpoint (Wp.5 18M) for spectacular (though rather vertiginous) views down the **Metade Valley** and **Faja da Noguiera** on a clear day.

If your vertigo allows, and if the day is cloud-free, you can continue to a second viewpoint another fifteen minutes farther on, with views to **Funchal**.

The return from either viewpoint can feel most enervating at this altitude, making the stone seats provided alongside the path up from the knoll most welcome.

The viewpoints are a simple way of testing your head for heights, before committing yourself to the long mountain routes, such as **Arieiro** to **Pico Ruivo** to **Encumeada**.

... views, views ...

The **São Lourenço** peninsula is Madeira's wild, often windy and always mysterious eastern tip, where sheer cliffs face the full force of the Atlantic Ocean.

An unusual 'bare rock' style of walk by Madeiran standards, this is one of the island's 'must do' routes and is a popular guided walk.

The bare rock peninsula of São Lourenço

Once an 'experts only' route to reach the far side of the **Estreito** 'straights', sturdy steel poles rigged with steel hawsers (far sturdier than the many steel wires seen on *levadas*) now guide walkers over this previously difficult section. Please note that the low to medium vertigo risk increases dramatically if you go to the cliff edges at the *miradouro* view points.

Access by car:
There's a large car park at the end of the ER-109 at the start of the route.

Access by bus:
Take the N°113 bus service from **Machico** and **Caniçal**, to its terminus at the large car park at the end of the ER-109.

We start out from the car park at the end of the ER-109 (Wp.1 0M) from where a well-trodden path drops down into the valley to a signboard which requests that we keep to official paths and respect the environment; from here, we go right to cross the valley floor (Wp.2). White posts mark the official route as we climb up the northern side of the valley on the stony path, with the **Pedras Brancas** trig point above us on the left. Our route levels out to run along to a stone wall and a second signboard (Wp.3 10M). Twin paths take us past the next white post (Wp.4), to curve around the hillside to a path crossroads (Wp.5 16M).

On the left is a cliff-edge *miradouro*, while on the right a path leads down to a pebble beach on the **Baía da Abra**. Over the crossroads, we start climbing over rock to reach a white post (Wp.6), more posts and cairns guiding us onto a clear path (Wp.7 23M) before more climbing to a crest (Wp.8). Our route follows the posts and cairns, undulating along and then starting a short descent (Wp.9) before contouring round to a *miradouro* viewpoint (Wp.10 30M) overlooking the **Pedra Furada** 'sea horse' rocks (see the photo over page).

The path now runs across a saddle to a junction (Wp.11) with another *miradouro* viewpoint, a few metres to our left, and then undulates along,

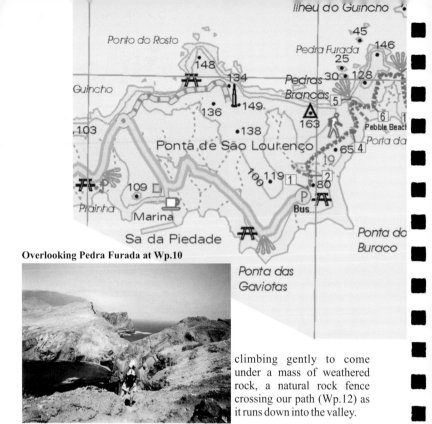

Overlooking Pedra Furada at Wp.10

climbing gently to come under a mass of weathered rock, a natural rock fence crossing our path (Wp.12) as it runs down into the valley.

Coming to the end of the rock section (Wp.13), we swing left into a gentler grassed valley, crossing its dry watercourse (Wp.14 40M) before turning out of the valley to come above cliffs and fish farms. A gentle climb brings us up to the stone marker on the summit of the ridge (Wp.15 45M), its northern side plunging down to the ocean.

From just below the summit, sturdy steel posts linked by steel hawsers give us safe guidance across the previously difficult **Estreito** section, which looks trickier from the top of the ridge than it is when we actually pick our way down over the rock

Looking down on Casa do Sardinha

A second post and hawser section brings us (gratefully) down the lava rock onto a non-vertiginous path which leads us across to a *miradouro* viewpoint at the head of the cliffs (Wp.16 56M).

As the path progresses east, we overlook the valley before **Casa do Sardinha** at a path junction (Wp.17), where we have a choice of a clockwise

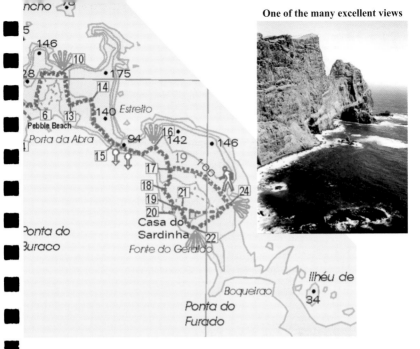

One of the many excellent views

or an anticlockwise tour encircling the house. We go down to the right (anticlockwise), and look back to take in the impressive views of the undercut cliffs below our 'post and hawser' traverse.

As we descend, we pass a marker post (Wp.18), more posts guiding us down to a junction (Wp.19 65M) and on to overlook the tiny quay which serves the house (Wp.20), where steps lead down to the sea for (optional) bathing.

Turning away from the quay, we take the path up towards the house, originally built as a hideaway for a **Funchal** businessman, but now occupied by park rangers. We go right at a junction (Wp.21) to reach a cliff-top viewpoint (Wp.22) before the path curves above **Casa do Sardinho** (Wp.23 80M). We pass another viewpoint (Wp.24) before arriving back at the junction with our outward route (Wp.17).

There's only one way back, and the 'post and hawser' traverse seems steeper in this direction. Retracing our outward route gives us a second chance to pause at the *miradouros* to experience the remarkable cliffs and rock formations plunging down to a deep blue sea.

... remarkable cliffs and rock formations ...

Levada do Caniçal (west) is a classical-style *levada* walking route in the east of the island which combines easy walking with impressive flora. It's a popular route, so start early in the morning, or leave it to the afternoon if you want to avoid the crowds. There's a slight vertigo risk in sections alongside unguarded drops early on, but after that, it's easy.

Access by bus or taxi: *Bar O Túnel**, off route

Get to the start of this linear route on bus N°156 bus from **Machico** or by taxi. Alight from the bus at its terminus near the top of **Maroços**. If arriving by taxi, ask for 'Levada do Caniçal'.

From the bus terminus near the top of **Maroços**, we could go over the river on a pedestrian bridge to face a long concrete stair leading up through the houses to reach the *levada*.

The levada at Wp.1

However, our choice is to continue up the village street to the water channel's start (Wp.1 0M), where the street now swings left to a junction with the new road, just before the tunnel. (Taxi users join us here.)

Houses in a variety of styles cling to the steep slopes, as we stroll along past a 'stair' access and a spring, before passing between houses randomly stacked up a promontory (Wp.2 6M) and a second spring, where the concrete gives way to a dirt *levada* path (Wp.3 10M).

Leaving the main houses behind,

we head up into a side valley towards tree-covered slopes, the croaking of frogs coming up from pools in the valley floor. As we turn into a pocket in the valley wall the croaking becomes almost deafening as we cross the line of a watercourse before going over the **Ribeira das Cales** watercourse and heading back towards the main valley. Above a yellow house, the path surface is concrete again (Wp.4 22M), though it is slightly vertiginous until we come between houses to swing left across the access stair for another promontory stacked with houses (Wp.5). A dirt and stone path now takes us into a pocket with a green 'wet bowl' at its head (28M).

Cultivated plots line the *levada* as we come back to the main valley, to cross stair access ways above a school, then turning our backs on the new tunnel (Wp.6 35M) we come into the **Ribeira Grande** valley. The path is concreted, handrails protecting the previously unguarded drops. We pass a substantial spring (Wp.7) and some cute houses before reaching a bridge at the head of a sharp valley (Wp.8 47M); here, fruit is offered for sale, and a sign announces, 'Moroços 3km, O Túnel do Caniçal 9km'.

Back on a dirt path, we head back towards the main valley through trees, a rickety guard rail covering a small landslip section, soaring pines and eucalyptus announcing our turn into the main valley. We walk through a small valley shaded by mimosa trees, passing plots that are in cultivation, even though we are some distance from the nearest houses. Continuing on our path, we go past a water tap and a trio of houses with 'healthy' stair access for the fit, followed a while later by a cave and then a tunnel (Wp.9 58M); no torch required.

Our route has taken us away from housing for some time, but all this changes when we pass a hut astride the *levada* (Wp.10 61M) and our route turns into

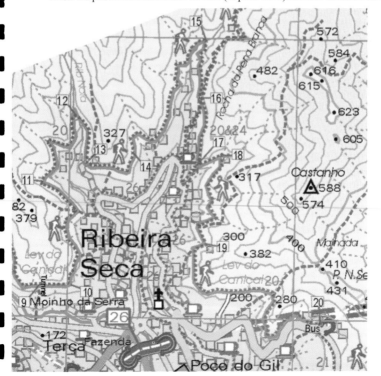

the populated valley of **Ribeira Seca**. Plots below the water channel are still in cultivation, while those at our altitude are abandoned; then we continue strolling through the beautiful natural landscape to cross a watercourse (Wp.11 72M), a popular stopping place for groups of walkers in this picturesque setting. We come to the first cultivated plots at *levada* level that we've seen for some time, before crossing the **Ribeira da Noia** watercourse (Wp.12 85M) below the channel, then coming onto the *levada* path once more.

Overlooking the valley of Ribeira Seca

On turning out of the valley there is the surprising sight of a levada-side warehouse served by a road (Wp.13 92M), as we curve round to overlook the valley of **Ribeira Seca** and its extensive housing. Now we head into the **Ribeira Seca** valley, the path's concrete surface replaced by dirt (Wp.14 96M), a sign that we're moving away from housing.

Development thins out the further we progress through the tranquil landscape and up the valley, to cross the watercourse by a public tap (Wp.15 111M) and head back towards more populous regions. Shortly, we pass the **Boca do Risco** path as it crosses the *levada* (Wp.16 117M) and come rapidly above cottages, as the valley becomes intensively housed along its access road. After passing our **Boca do Risco** outward route (Wp.17 Walk 24) our surroundings become rural once again as the path turns into a side pocket, turning below rock steps that lead up to a large hut (Wp.18 126M). Coming back into the main valley, we cross two streams in small pockets, then pass through a stand of eucalyptus and pines before passing below two 'weekender' huts in a intensively terraced pocket (Wp.19 136M).

Mimosa woods and a change to red earth herald our swinging round to come above the **Caniçal** road where a section of concrete path curves left towards houses ahead. **Bar/Restaurante O Túnel** is below us - take the downward path if you want to finish at the bar - just before we pass new houses and go between more houses to reach the end of the open *levada* alongside the road, tunnel entrance and bus stop (Wp.20 158M).

From here, we have the choice of catching the N°113 bus back to **Machico**, heading up the road opposite on our Walk 21 'Peak and Town' route to **Machico**, or strolling down the road to **Bar/Restaurante O Túnel** for refreshments, before deciding our onward course.

Meeting the road at Wp.20

The view west from Pico do Facho

Pico do Facho (323 metres) not only offers us a superb viewpoint over the eastern coastline of Madeira, the **São Lourenço** peninsula, and the **Ilhas Desertas**, it also makes you feel like King Kong, as 'toy-sized' aircraft seem close enough to pluck out of the sky as they make their landing approach to the airport.

* in **Machico**

Access by bus:
Take the Nº113 **Machico-Caniçal** bus. The route is also a natural extension of Walk 20.

From the entrance to the **Caniçal** tunnel (Wp.1 0M), we set off up the **Pico do Facho** road. It's an energetic, steady ascent, rewarded by increasing panoramas over the **Machico** valley as we climb past the green gates of a water treatment site to the right, followed by a scruffy construction yard on the right, and even a cottage with its own fire engine on our left.

We reach the point where the old **Machico-Caniçal** donkey trail crosses the road (Wp.2 18M), some fifteen metres before an electricity pylon.

Machico, seen from the peak

We continue slogging up the steep tarmac road, with views now opening up over **Caniçal** (Wp.3), before we turn right and come up to the parking area below **Pico do Facho**. Pathways take us up the slopes below the transmitter to find a suitable vantage point (Wp.4 23M).

The donkey trail at Wp.2

When we are satiated with the views (0M), we head back down the road - far easier down than up, of couse - until we reach the **Machico-Caniçal** donkey trail again (Wp.2 5M), below the electricity pylon. Here, we leave the tarmac to start dropping down the rough boulder trail, often hidden by long grass, to come alongside a stone wall.

Our path divides (Wp.5 8M) and we go right and down across the sloping meadow, the trail now more stone than grass. Coming below a small rock outcrop (Wp.6 12M), we take the left path. Our trail, at times a narrow river of rubble, angles down across the meadow, and then curves right to drop towards the large *residência* building which has cut the old trail, where we have to go left alongside the fencing to drop down onto a 'new' road (Wp.7 26M) alongside the *residência*.

From here, you could drop steeply down the **Caminho da Quinta Palmeira** into **Banda de Além**, but we go left along the 'new' **Estrada de Misericórdia** road, for a gentler but longer descent. It is an easy stroll along above houses before we drop down to meet the old port road (Wp.**8**) where we go right to stroll beneath stately plane trees and on into the **Banda de Além** square by the bridge (Wp.9 46M), where we are close to a choice of bar/restaurants for refreshments.

Few people realise that the **Levada do Caniçal** continues beyond the road tunnel. While the start (beneath a quarry) and finish (down a featureless road) are unimpressive the main part of our route is through beautiful countryside and woodland which has escaped the depredations of **Caniçal**'s expansion and the new bridge works.

Time and a small forest fire have conspired to close the alternative to the 'Levada Bridge', the small valley is now stuffed with briars, so be prepared to get your feet/footwear wet.

*in **Caniçal**

Access by Bus:
Bus access on N°113 **Machico-Caniçal** bus route, or as an extension of Walk 20 by walking through the road tunnel.

Stairs at the eastern end of the road tunnel lead up to a shrine while lower down, the **Levada do Caniçal** leaves the road (Wp.1 0M). You can either follow the canal from this point to traverse a handrail section, or go down the main road, then walk up the quarry access road to gain the *levada* (Wp.2 4M).

After crossing a watercourse, we move along below the quarry's rock wall to negotiate a narrow section with an unprotected drop; concentrating on your footsteps means you should notice the '1955' date in the channel's wall.

Fine views early in the route

Passing a falling rocks sign (12M) our path runs along a boulder wall before we tackle another unprotected drop where the *levada* and path clings to a cliff face.

Rounding a bluff (Wp.3 17M), the path improves as we head north across grassy slopes before turning into the **Cova Grande** valley by a water change point (20M).

The *levada* becomes piped as we cross the valley's watercourse on a substantial concrete water runoff (Wp.4 24M).

Shortly, the *levada* reverts to running water as we curve

Curving north above Caniçal

Fine views to São Lourenço from the *levada*

north above the uppermost houses of **Caniçal**, fine views from our elevated position over the **São Lourenço** peninsula.

The hillside becomes steeper and wilder as we curve into another valley, while ahead are huts and cultivated terraces served by a dirt road

... steeper and wilder ...

that climbs up the valley and replaces the *levada* path (Wp.5 30M).

Below a large hut with a noisy dog, we leave the dirt road to follow the water channel before swinging left into a tree-filled valley.

We stroll through the trees to come to a small *levada* bridge over the valley's watercourse (Wp.6 37M); once there was a choice of how to cross the valley but impenetrable briars now mean that wading across in the water is our only option (sandals an advantage over boots); but in this beautiful woodland, it's no hardship to take a few minutes 'drying out' after the crossing.

Wading through the water

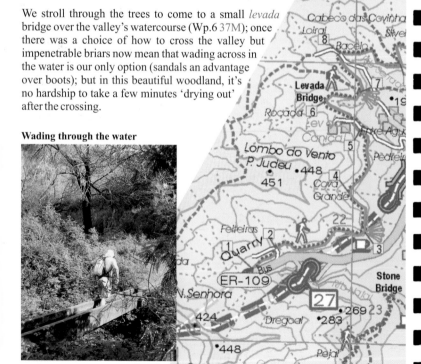

From the bridge, we stroll through the flower-filled woodland to come out of the trees to views over the peninsula (Wp.7 41M), our route now curving through open woodland into another valley. Across the valley floor, the *levada* heads out of the valley and past the remains of huts and terraces and a water runoff bridged over the watercourse.

We swing into another tree-filled valley where the water channel is edged with a riot of flowers. Across the valley's watercourse and a dirt track (Wp.8,) the plants now almost overwhelm the channel, requiring careful footwork to avoid stepping in the water.

All too soon this floriferous valley changes to open woodland, a small culvert taking water down the hillside on our right (Wp.9 58M) shortly before the *levada* swings right to run downhill beside a dirt road (Wp.10 62M).

Our final stage is an easy stroll down the dirt road above water eroded slopes. Past a domed water reservoir and with the industrial zone fence on our left, the track becomes a tarmac lane heading down past the first houses, where we come onto a a

The quirky Whale Bar

junction beside the *correios* (post office) (Wp.11 80M) with the 'end of motorway' roundabout on our left.

Straight over the junction, we follow a town street down past the 'whale' bar (closed) and new church as it swings right to come down to the centre of **Caniçal** by its old church, bus stop, taxis and some well-earned refreshments at **Bar Moreira** (Wp.12 84M), a bar so laid back, it's almost supine.

There was a time before the ER-109 road when the main access to **Caniçal** was by donkey trail over the **Facho** ridge. Standing in **Machico** it looks a daunting prospect, but with a little effort you can enjoy the wild landscapes between these two towns. Our 'main route' from the tunnel entrance will save you a considerable climb. The old path is now little walked and even less maintained, a shame as it takes us through delightful countryside; take secateurs to keep the route open (trousers more comfortable than shorts), beware of eroded sections of path.

Access by bus:

N°113 bus to **Túnel do Caniçal** entrance. Return on the N°113 bus from **Caniçal**.

*in **Caniçal**

Alternative start from **Machico** (add 1 walker, 30 minutes and 230 metres of ascents)

We start out from **Machico** to cross over the bridge into **Banda de Além** square, where we go left to walk up the narrow street. At **Auto Milagres** we turn right to climb steeply up to meet another street and then turn downhill to another junction, with a water tap, where we turn left. Now we face a puff and grunt, slogging ascent up the steep road past a school to come to the T-junction in front of the impressive **Residencia**; this first ascent on tarmac streets is the worst of the whole route which makes the climb up the donkey trail seem comparatively easy. Now we go up the right side of the large building to come onto the boulder-laid trail showing through the long grass. It is another energetic ascent as our trail curves left diagonally across the steep meadow, before swinging right for another diagonal ascent towards an electricity pylon. Another lazy climbing zigzag, left then right below a rock outcrop, brings us above the first pylon to a crumbling boulder wall. Now we are climbing up alongside the wall towards a pylon on the ridge, the boulder-laid trail replaced by a twisting dirt

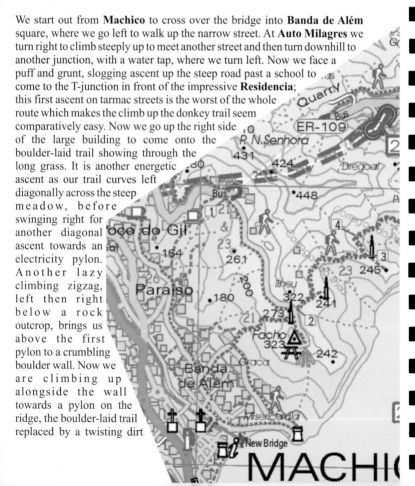

path that climbs up onto the **Pico do Facho** road (Wp.2 48M); from this point adjust your timings for the 'official' route. After that steep relentless climb you might take a diversion up to picnic area below the peak before continuing on to **Caniçal**.

Official start from Túnel do Caniçal
Alighting from the N°113 bus at the start of the **Pico do Facho** road (Wp.1 0M) we stride up the tarmac leaving the houses behind, the gradient steepening to bring us to a yard on our right, then passing below a cottage with a fire tender in its drive. After 'creaking frog pond' in an old quarry, we're ascending again to meet the 'old Caniçal' path which crosses the road by a pylon (Wp.2 18M).

Our track heading north-east

It's quite a slog up the road, but we recommend continuing ascending to the picnic area below **Pico do Facho** to enjoy the views down over **Machico** and landing approach, airliners passing beneath us as they come into the airport, though add 20 minutes for this diversion as walk timings are for continuous walking from Wp.2.

Our track gently descends (NE) as it curves around the hillside to a junction. Ignoring a track off to the right we curve (N) as the track narrows to a path above the steep **Corrego do Ilhéu** valley and a pylon. The path drops down quite steeply before levelling out below traditional huts, then crossing the bowl of the valley above the steep cleft down to the sea. Ahead, a pylon surmounts a bare ridge and our path starts climbing gently through tree-dotted slopes towards it, getting narrower and steeper for us to push through tall heather to come onto the promontory beside the pylon (Wp.3 42M), an excellent if windy viewpoint over the rugged coastal landscape.

At the pylon our path has a discontinuity on the bare

rock and it's easy to think the onward route is down the line of the ridge, but no! Facing the pylon, our correct path is left and behind us to drop down along the northern side of the ridge. Our narrow, eroded path drops down through mimosa trees to emerge between long abandoned terraces as we cross the valley's watercourse (Wp.4 49M). Stone walls guide us round a rocky ridge into a smaller, steeper valley notable for its rock walls. Our path narrows for a picky descent seawards before turning (NE) towards **Caniçal**. When the path divides at a sheet of rock (old red paint waymark) we stay on the upper path for a gentle ascent along the top of a boulder wall. Coming alongside a rock outcrop the peninsula again comes into view; on rounding the outcrop we're looking down on **Caniçal** (Wp.5 74M). Our path runs inland below the outcrop before descending in zigzags, the route confirmed by old red waymarks.

... across grassy slopes ...

Over a stone ridge, our path now runs inland across grassy slopes to round a cleft slashed into the hillside before continuing down past old walls, coming above the pebble beach at the mouth of the **Ribeira Natal** valley where the stone bridge comes into view (Wp.6 93M); if walking the route in reverse make sure you keep right at this point as continuing straight ahead leads to an impressive dead-end at the top of cliffs. Our path becomes rockier, requiring concentration, as we drop towards the valley floor, a steep scrambling descent finally bringing us down to the stone bridge over the watercourse (Wp.7 103M).

Looking back from the stone bridge

A few metres of path bring us onto the tarmac road serving the beach. Previously we faced a stiff climb up the road out of the valley, but now we turn downhill to stroll down to the mini yacht club and bar (Wp.8 106M). After refreshment (optional but recommended) we stroll along the new but rather neglected beach-front promenade which leads us to **Caniçal**'s road system (Wp.9) where we stroll down past a seafront swimming pool to new seafront parking. A left turn and a short climb take us up to **Bar Moreira** conveniently situated alongside the bus stop and taxis (Wp.10 121M).

The 'Dangerous Gateway', **Boca do Risco**, is a popular walking destination, with its fine views along Madeira's rugged north coast. Beyond the 'gate', the path soon becomes seriously vertiginous, and we only recommend taking this route to descend to **Porto da Cruz** as part of a guided walking group.

The route up to **Boca do Risco** is straightforward, but the path is narrow and slightly vertiginous in places and can become slippery in wet weather, so we recommend this as a dry weather walk only.

3 | 3H | 10 km | 270m / 270m | ↻ | 1-2 | 2*

*in **Machico or Ribeira Seca**

N.B. This information bar refers to the full route when starting from **Machico**.

Access by car:
Car drivers can park on **Machico** sea front parking, or drive up to **Ribeiro Seco** to park on the entrance road, for the shorter walk option.

The shorter option
From **Machico**, the easiest option is to catch the N°113 (**Caniçal**) bus. As the bus climbs up the valley wall past the **O Crespo** bar (on our right) to round a hairpin bend, press the bell; the bus will stop at the entrance road to **Ribeiro Seco**. (2 hours, 7 kilometres, 200 metres ascents & descents)

The full route from Machico

Starting from **Machico** church square (Wp.1 0M), we walk over the bridge into the square of **Banda da Além**, where we turn left. We take the second street on the right, to climb steeply up to a junction, at which we turn left to follow the street to **Ribeiro Seco**. It is an easy stroll along the almost traffic-free street, lined by houses ranging from basic to intricate; look out for the unusual dwelling decorated with lots of pottery figures (Wp.2). The houses become more obviously affluent as we pass **Bar Migaro** (Wp.3), shortly before a final climb up to cross the main road (Wp.4 30M).

Passing bar/shop **Larano** (0M), we stroll into **Ribeiro Seco** along a street of diverse local architecture where one section of housing built against the steep valley wall could be christened, 'extreme driveways', before we pass through an old bus turning circle (Wp.5) and then stroll gently down to the **Bar Boca do Risco** (Wp.6 12M).

Now the climbing starts in earnest as we take a concrete stair opposite the bar, to ascend steeply over a cross-roads of paths and come behind a cottage (Wp.7). From the cottage, we climb up on a steep dirt path which becomes a rock 'stair' before we pass vegetable plots and then climb steep concrete steps to reach the broad

Bar Boca do Risco at Wp.6

path alongside the **Levada do Caniçal** (Wp.8 23M). This section of the route is so steep that we recommend it only for ascending to the *levada*, not as a descent.

We now have an easy stroll (N) along the *levada* path, overlooking the conventional route which trudges up the valley past isolated cottages to cross the water channel (Wp.9 28M). Leaving the *levada*, our stone-laid trail climbs steadily past a hut and terraces to pass through a grove of mimosas, then curving above cultivated terraces and huts (Wp.10).

Our path is a narrow brown ribbon which contours above the plots before it curves into a sharp cleft in the valley wall. Crossing the watercourse (Wp.11 40M), our path runs over rocks before curving back to wind through the tall pines which line the main valley. Our route swings right into another pine-filled pocket, beautiful wild hillside above us as we cross the watercourse (Wp.12) to climb above the trees, as we come back into the main valley.

In this wild, natural landscape, it is a surprise to come up to face an 'oil drum' smallholding (Wp.13 51M) where 'Boca do Risco' is signed left along a narrow dirt path which requires careful footwork through intrusive vegetation.

Soon, though, we are back to heading north on a good path, for the long, steady climb up to the natural gate in the cliff top ridge that is **Boca do Risco** (Wp.14 58M). We pass through the *boca*, and just beyond it are rewarded with spectacular views (on a clear day) along Madeira's the northern coastline.

A well-earned rest after Wp.14

The northern coastal path beyond **Boca do Risco** descends along the vertiginous cliff face to the steep agricultural settlement of **Larano**. If you wish to walk this route, we suggest joining a guided group; even the most experienced mountain walkers should only attempt the route in good weather and not forget this quote from a recent walker, "… the most dangerous and vertiginous path we used all week.".

After taking in the views (and perhaps a picnic), we return by the same route, again with careful footwork on the narrow sections of path, to the **Levada do Caniçal**. From the *levada*, we take the traditional path for a steady descent past cottages into the valley. The path becomes concrete at an ugly concrete building (Wp.15), twisting down between houses before coming into the open again. At a yellow house, the path twists steeply down between the buildings to drop us onto the road (Wp.16) near the junction with the new valley road.

If your car is parked near the ER-109 road, then go left past **Bar O'Pasta** (Wp.17) to join your outward route at **Bar Boca do Risco**. Those who walked from **Machico** have the option of returning the same way, or of taking the new road down the valley to follow the lower roads back to the church square.

Portela, with its views, *tipico* catering, parking, taxi rank and bus stop, has all the desired attributes for a walking base. However, few guide books use this approach to the area, choosing to simply arrive from **Ribeira Frio** or depart for **Porto da Cruz**. This is their loss, as we embark on a circular route that offers options for you to extend your woodland walking on three recently waymarked trails, and bus users could opt for a less energetic finish at **Ribeira de Machico**.

* plus extensions

Access by bus:
Bus access on N°53 or 78 service.

> **Short Option**
> Follow the dirt road to Wp.9, then take the forest path back to Wp.6 and return to **Portela** on the dirt road (2 hours).

Access by car:
Car drivers can park on the side road off the **Portela** junction.

Main Circular Route
If arriving by bus, jump off at the **Portela** bus stop. Drivers should park along the side road off the **Portela** junction.

Starting out from the **Bar/Rest Miradouro da Portela** (Wp.1 0M), we stroll along the tarmac lane (E), accompanied by the narrow **Levada da Portela**, enjoying views down the northern valley to **Porto da Cruz** and to the mountainous bulk of **Águia**.

Where the tarmac lane swings right (2M) signed, 'Ribeira do Machico 2km', we go ahead on a dirt road, past a path off to our left signed, 'Portela - Cruz de Guarda caminho municipal'.

Our route is lined with fine specimens of mature pines, the tiny *levada* on our right, as we come to a *miradouro* viewpoint (Wp.2 12M) overlooking the north coast. We pass a water-filled tunnel bored into the hillside (Wp.3), earth steps climbing the hillside beside it.

The *levada* goes through a tunnel (Wp.4 17M) while we follow the dirt

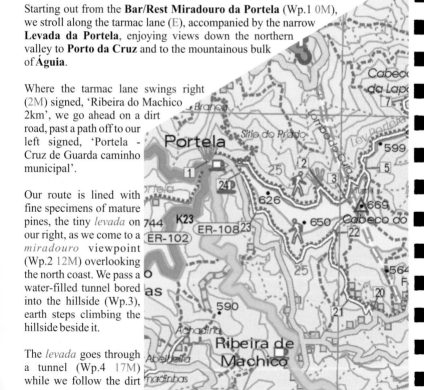

The *levada* tunnel at Wp.4

road round the promontory to rejoin the channel shortly before a track climbs up the hillside (Wp.5) to service a transmitter station; a short circular route option over the peak to Wp.22.

The plant life in this region is so vigorous that it unfortunately denies us clear views, as we gently stroll along the dirt road to arrive at a 'Serra das Funduras' signboard (Wp.6 27M).

Miradouru views en route

A path beside the sign goes into the forest, the first of three laurel forest trails that have been created in this conservation area. If you choose to take this trail, you will rejoin our route in 2½ kilometres at Wp.9.

We continue along the dirt road (better GPS coverage than in the forest), past access to terraces below us, leading to a *miradouro* viewpoint for more superb views (Wp.7 32M). Dark cliffs spring up alongside our route before more views (42M), and further views can be enjoyed where a dirt road goes left onto a mound on a spur (Wp.8 45M).

Here, the route swings right to climb steadily between tree-covered slopes. Five minutes of uphill takes us over the crest of the road, to look down into the **Machico** valley. We drop down past moss-covered earth banks and cycads, giving testimony to the wetter climate this side of the ridge. As we swing left, we find ahead the sign, 'Serra das Funduras' at the end of the laurel forest path (Wp.9 60M).

For the Short Route
At the sign for 'Serra das Funduras' turn onto the laurel forest path (Wp.9) and return to Wp.6.

Continuation of the Main Circular Route
We continue downhill through a cutting, and come to the second forest trail at a hairpin bend (Wp.10 62M) where there is a picnic table beneath a shelter sited above the bend; the second laurel forest trail starts from the shelter. Staying on the dirt road, we follow it down into the valley to a T-junction where we go right (Wp.11 70M); if you were to go left at this junction, you would come to the end of the second forest trail, followed by the third forest trail.

After all that downhill our road now contours around the valley wall, from where we look out over to the houses around **Maroços**, and then runs downhill to cross a watercourse before climbing to a crest and descending through the forest again.

Periwinkle thrives on the route

Endemic flora are prolific alongside the forest road with some classic sized ferns and cycads in the wetter pockets of this section amongst the wild flowers.

We pass a wooden hut below the dirt road (Wp.12 89M) and then an earth bank decorated with carved graffiti, before swinging left across a watercourse (Wp.13 93M). Our route runs gently uphill to pass a dirt road which runs down into the valley on our left, and at the next watercourse crossing (Wp.14 97M) is another 'Zona das Funduras' signboard. As we walk up the gentle incline, we pass a shrine carved into the earth bank (Wp.15) before swinging across another watercourse.

We pass a dirt road off to our left (Wp.16) and can see our first house ahead through the trees.; after passing another dirt road on our left which drops into the valley, we come uphill to gates by a house (Wp.17 109M). Shortly after passing another dirt road off to the left, we swing right to the unlikely sight of a 'pink marzipan' cottage. Now street lights accompany us past the pink house and another dirt road off to the left (Wp.18) before reaching a garage where civilisation in the form of a tarmac lane begins.

Swinging right, we climb gently on the lane past a scattering of houses, to the unlikely sight of a small bar (Wp.19 120M). 'Support your rural bar', is our motto, dictating a stop for canned drinks and doing our bit to help this marginal establishment to stay in business for those walkers that come after us, thirsty after two hours in the forest.

From the spartan bar (0M) we continue to go gently uphill to the crest of the lane by a new house, and then amble downhill past 'treasure chest' crash barriers, passing two modern houses before we turn right onto a concrete, then dirt road (Wp.20 12M). Bus users not relishing the invigorating 150 metre ascent back to **Portela** should see the alternative finish**.

Remembering all that downhill walking, it is no surprise that we must face a 'puff and grunt' ascent up the steep, badly eroded dirt road. We climb up through two hairpin bends before the gradient moderates as we pass an old cottage on our right and then come to a pair of houses (Wp.21 21M).

At the corner of the houses the dirt road goes right and we walk up past a shanty house on the right, with chained and caged vicious dogs alongside our route; do not try to pet these animals, simply put them behind you and head up to the forested slopes.

Our steady ascent on the red earth road continues up to a T-junction (Wp.22 31M) amongst mimosas and towering eucalyptus.

Ascending amongst mimosas

The dirt road to the right climbs steeply up to the transmitter on the peak (see Wp.5), but we go left and climb gently through a hairpin bend, to stroll along with traffic sounds drifting up to us from the **Portela** road. You'll recognise 'big boulder' corner (Wp.23 40M), shortly before the dirt road runs out onto a tarmac road (Wp.24 45M). Going right brings us back onto our outward route, just a few metres from our start point (48M). If you would prefer your refreshments alfresco, head down the **Machico** road to the lower bar/restaurant with its outdoor tables.

** Alternative finish for bus users.
Instead of climbing the dirt road at Wp.20 continue along the tarmac lane. At a T-junction go right, towards **Ribeira de Machico**, to another T-junction. This time go left, **Portela** is signed right, to walk up to the ER-108 'main road' in **Ribeira de Machico** where you will find bar and bus stop.

Madeira is a green island and to state the obvious, this is because it receives plenty of rain water. Previously walkable paths become slippery, cloying mud. Accessible *levadas* are deluged by cascades of water, making routes dangerous. When it is too wet for country walking, it's good to have an 'all weather' reserve route, with plenty of *tipicos* to choose from, while waiting for the island to dry out.

Starting out from the main square in **Machico** (Wp.1 0M), we walk over the bridge into the other square of **Banda de Além** (Wp.2), where we turn left to head inland along the cobbled street. At the health food shop, we turn right to head up a steep street with the sign, 'Aluvião 3/11/1956' on its corner (3M). The steep climb takes us up to a junction by a public water point, where we turn left and continue uphill (NNW).

At this junction, you could stay on the road to follow it straight up to rejoin the route at *.

After forty metres, we turn right to climb another steep street (NE) which gets noticeably steeper as we come up to a blue painted wall covered with graffiti at its top (12M). We head left (WNW) on a narrow tarmac lane that runs between houses and soon becomes a concrete path running along a contour at the upper limit of **Machico**'s housing development.

We cross the route of our Walk 23 'The Old Trail to Caniçal' walk (15M) just below the highest developments in town, as we head north on the concrete walkway. Traditional huts are set below the path, just before we turn into a cleft where a small concrete bridge takes us over the watercourse (17M).

The path crosses the top of a steep cobbled lane just before we come to a modern house with double gates and garage - but just how do you get a car to it? Our elevated stroll continues through the higher houses, some decorated with traditional roof corner tiles of birds of angels, with views down over the populated valley below us on our left.

The path ends at a long concrete stairway overlooking a sharp cleft (25M), where we go left down the stairs to come onto a tarmac lane which is bridged over the cleft and its watercourse.

Corner roof detail

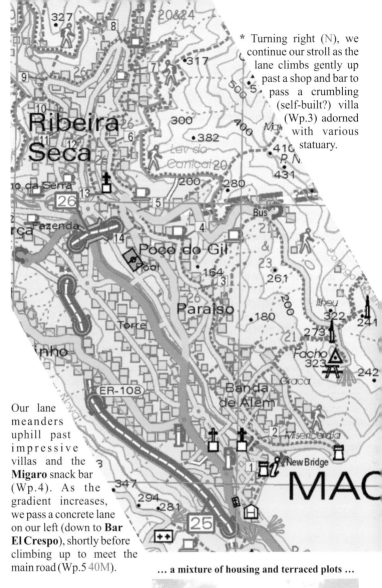

* Turning right (N), we continue our stroll as the lane climbs gently up past a shop and bar to pass a crumbling (self-built?) villa (Wp.3) adorned with various statuary.

Our lane meanders uphill past impressive villas and the **Migaro** snack bar (Wp.4). As the gradient increases, we pass a concrete lane on our left (down to **Bar El Crespo**), shortly before climbing up to meet the main road (Wp.5 40M).

... a mixture of housing and terraced plots ...

We cross carefully over the main road to walk up a tarmac lane past **Entrado de Larano** shop and bar, and a gentle uphill stroll takes us into the **Ribeira Seca** valley past a mixture of housing and terraced plots.

Although from a distance this area seems to be made up of identikit modern houses, but at close quarters we see the diversity of designs, many incorporating a certain degree of quirkiness. For example, a house below the bus stop (Wp.6) has a rooftop parking area accessed by a 45° semi-staired driveway. We pass up through an old bus turning circle, then the lane runs gently downhill for a while.

There are plenty of refreshment stops along the way as the route undulates along the valley wall; for example, we come to **Bar Boca da Risco** (Wp.7) opposite the stairway route of Walk 24. Another couple of minutes brings us past **Bar O Pastel** to a road junction at the head of the valley (Wp.8 57M). Here, a new road has been built down the valley, giving us an alternative but less interesting route.

We now begin to move along the western wall amongst the mix of building styles and quirkiness before passing the steep **Caminho Municipal de Nóia** (Wp.9 66M) which goes up to our right. We've passed a few bars along the route, but now we meet a 'Mexican stand-off' as **Bar Stop** faces **Bar Parada** across the narrow street (Wp.10 70M); if you can't choose between them, you can always move on to the next bar (Wp.11 73M), where a road drops steeply down to our left - this is the continuation of our route. Alternatively, you could continue along the western valley wall on the street and pick up the valley roads back to **Machico**.

We take the steep road left for a skittering descent past a school, to come onto the new valley road (Wp.12). Over the road, we come onto a walkway across the watercourse, to walk along to a tarmac lane and steps, which bring us up to a church (Wp.13). In front of its façade (refurbished in 1999), we walk across the ornately cobbled square onto the tarmac street that takes us up to the main road.

A few metres down the road, we cross carefully over to drop into **Bar O'Crespo** (Wp.14 87M); this artistic, new style *tipico* (with excellent coffee) contrasts with the traditional bars encountered so far. At the side of **Bar O'Crespo**, a concrete lane takes us up to rejoin our outward route below the main road, from where it is all downhill strolling back to **Banda de Além** and **Machico**.

Encumeada is the pass in Madeira's centre from which great gorges carve their way down to the north (**São Vicente**) and south (**Ribeira Brava**) coasts. The pass, and its bar, mark the finish for the seriously expert route which comes from **Pico Ruivo**, but today we follow the simplest of routes, enjoying the flora and views along the manicured **Levada do Norte**.

Access by car:
Arriving at **Encumeada**, turn onto the ER-110 and park opposite the gewgaw shop, and walk back down the road to **Bar Encumeada**. Please do not park at the bar unless you are a customer.

Access by bus:
Buses are very few, N° 6 or 139, to **Encumeada** pass. Don't make the mistake of getting off at the **Residencial Encumeada** or you'll face a long slog up the road to the pass.

WEST (30-40 minutes)
On the start of the route west

Steps across the road from the bar take us up onto the broad path, signed 'Folhada', which accompanies the **Levada do Norte** (Wp.1 0M) to walk west against the water flow.

We pass beneath the *levada* keeper's house, excellent flora lining the canal as we stroll along to a filtration point (Wp.2 5M).

Miradouro views open up over the valley and the **Residencial Encumeada** hotel (Wp.3), before we reach a water run-off where the channel goes underground for twenty-five metres (Wp.4), and we come to a second water run-off bridged over the *levada* (Wp.5).

Handrails protect a non-vertiginous section, even though it is far safer than some earlier sections, just before a broad area beside the canal, **Lapa do Galho**,

Passing the western water house

where we enjoy more *miradouro* views down the valley (Wp.6) Past another water run-off with fine views, we come along to the tunnel entrance above a sealed track which comes up the hillside to the *levada* (Wp.7 15M).

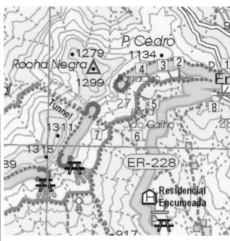

Extension for tunnel walkers
Tunnel walkers can tackle the ten to fifteen minute transit to the **Folhadal** - spectacular, rewarding us at its exit with magnificent laurisilva woodland, one of Madeira's last remaining examples of this ancient forest. We continue ahead through the woodland for approximately 10 minutes, with views over the **São Vicente** valley.

However, for our route today we continue beside the canal, now the **Levada das Rabaças**, until it swings right by a large pine (18M).

There is shaded space below the *levada* from which to take in the orogenical scenery from a seat on the rocks, before retracing our steps to **Bar Encumeada**.

EAST (20-30 minutes)

Views down to Residencial Encumeada

Behind the bar at **Encumeada**, we find the steps that take us up from the road (Wp.8 0M) and onto a garden-like path. The *levadeiros* have added plants to mingle with the endemic species, to create one of the most floriferous *levadas* on the island.

Lilies and hydrangeas blend with agapanthus and mimosa, as we stroll along beside the flowers enjoying extensive views down the **Serra da Agua** valley, (stopping to look at the view).

White agapanthus beside the route

After crossing a water runoff bridged over the *levada*, we encounter a holding tank, like a high altitude swimming pool (Wp.9 5M), which we edge round with the assistance of hand rails.

Across another water runoff, and then we have a flood runoff section with its triangular stepping stones and handrail (Wp.10), just before a *teleférico* hut.

The chocolate box cottage

We continue past a section with sturdy green hand rails (Wp.11), then come to a short, comfortable tunnel (Wp.12 10M) where a substantial green gate denies access outside 'normal' hours.

Beyond the tunnel is a neat *levada* keeper's 'chocolate box' cottage with a *miradouro* terrace; beside it, the waters of the *levada* churn into large holding tank.

The *miradouro* terrace

More substantial green railings protect the path alongside the holding tank, up to a sluice which sends the waters hurtling down the pipe to the **Serra da Agua** hydroelectric power station.

The views from anywhere by the cottage and holding tank are simply spectacular.

We return by the same route for refreshments in **Bar Encumeada**.

Madeira is dotted with isolated farm settlements where, far from centres of population, people wrested a living from the earth. Most of these settlements are long abandoned, nature reclaiming terraces which once supported a rural family. Today we visit **Curral Jangão**, set in picturesque surroundings on the **Ribeira do Poço** - an enjoyable woodland walk, almost untouched by modern civilisation.

Some sections of the path are narrow, requiring careful footwork, and there is a short, tricky descent/ascent to the hydro pipe.

Access by car:
As this is a linear 'there and back' route, it is best suited to car drivers. From the end of the **Via Rápida**, we head up the **Serra da Agua** valley to turn onto the ER-228 for **Encumeada**. A kilometre after passing the **Residencia Encumeada**, we turn right on a sharp left-hand bend, onto a dirt road, and park just off the tarmac (Wp.1 0M).

We set off down the rough track, our route confirmed by a signboard and fingerpost for the **PR12**, passing the tethered wire of the *teleférico* which serves the *levada* (Wp.2 5M), staying on the track until it runs out

The start of the route

(Wp.3 8M), where we continue on a stone-littered walking trail which plunges through broom and heather, to emerge on a clearer area with *miradouro* views down the valley (Wp.4 12M).

After pushing through more broom and heather before our path descends through eucalyptus, then dropping down a steep section of path (requiring care both on the outward and return routes) before we pass under a big hydro pipe (Wp.5 20M).

... dappled shade of eucalyptus ...

Our route now meanders along through the dappled shade of eucalyptus trees, a gentle downhill section bringing us to a rock area (Wp.6 28M); *miradouro* views from the rock outcrop off the path. We come back amongst trees to the sounds of running water, as our path runs into and out of pockets in the valley wall.

Three streams are crossed (taking care on the wet, slippery crossings, and on the narrower sections of the path), before we emerge from the trees to hillsides of heather, broom and bracken (Wp.7 40M).

After crossing a boulder-filled watercourse, we are gradually curving east into trees, crossing a tumbling stream and then emerging to views over the valley until yellow broom pushes in on our narrow path. Back under laurel trees, our path widens under the dappled shade and crosses a small stream below old terraces, before reaching a larger watercourse (Wp.8 50M).

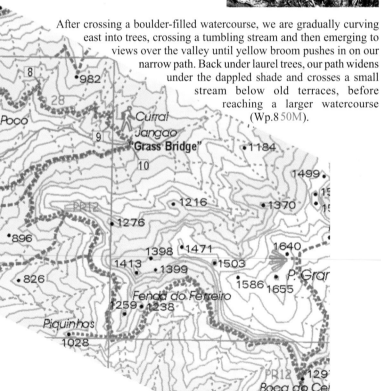

Views over the valley

A boulder-laid section of path climbs steadily and then curves left into the **Ribeiro do Poço** valley, to bring us back amongst woodland, with views of **Curral Jangão**'s abandoned terraces ahead.

We cross three more streams which follow clefts in the valley wall, more sections of boulder-laid path assisting us on the climbs.

The trail passes through spiky gorse and then deciduous trees, taking us to the remains of terraces (Wp.9 68M) as we walk above a hut.

Rushing water below us heralds our approach to a grass-covered stone bridge over the **Ribeira do Poço** (Wp.10 72M), the centrepiece of the **Curral Jangão**. If only there was some seating in the dappled shade, this beautiful location would be our favourite picnic location.

Extension
You can continue on the donkey trail from the Grass Bridge to finish at either **Boca da Corrida** or **Curral das Freiras**. See page 138 for map and details.

Bica da Cana is a popular weekend picnic site for the locals, when entire families spend the day barbecuing and relaxing amongst the tables and trees below the forest house. Some of them might venture as far as the 1640 metre trig point for its *miradouro* views, but few, if any, descend to the delights awaiting us on the **Levada da Serra**. This is a fine country walk on a picturesque *levada*, with sufficient descents and ascents for us to feel that the views have been well earned.

Access by car:
No bus access but plenty of roadside parking alongside the ER110 for car drivers.

We park alongside the road by the cooking and 'facilities' blocks (Wp.1 0M), and walk up between the trees and picnic tables to the main forestry building where a cobbled stair takes us up in the direction of the main peak and across a dirt road (Wp.2 5M). If you parked on the main road at the corner then walk up past the vehicle barrier on the dirt road and our routes meet at this point.

There are various paths, plus the dirt road, as alternatives for us to head up towards the peak, with vistas opening up around us as we reach a *miradouro* viewpoint and picnic tables at the end of the dirt road (Wp.3 8M).

After taking in the views, we climb up to the trig point (Wp.4 1640 metres), then we take a downhill path(s) towards the wind turbines. A dirt path joins us from the dirt road on our right, as we drop down alongside a fence to a stile (Wp.5 22M).

Now our path turns down alongside a watercourse (which we cross at Wp.6), to wind steeply down through the heather. The sound of bubbling water grows as we descend, until we drop down through steep zigzags onto the *levada* path by a faded 'Casa de Adrico de Caramujo' sign (Wp.7 36M).

Compared to the spartan descent through the heather, the *levada* is a different flower-bedecked world. We turn right to follow the water's flow beneath cliffs - slightly vertiginous - before the path widens and we reach a section of splashing waterfalls (Wp.8 40M). Flowers abound alongside the path, butterflies weaving amongst the flowers and water droplets, as we come to the main waterfall tumbling down the rock face, framed by its own rainbow (Wp.9 48M). Ahead is the jutting basalt outcrop of **Pináculo**; you can progress along the *levada* path, depending both upon the flow of the waterfalls which soak the route, and on your head for heights on the cliff section before **Pináculo**.

After enjoying the combination of running and falling water in this wild garden setting, we retrace our steps to the path junction (Wp.7 0M) and continue on to explore the *levada* in the opposite direction. Water drops down, feeding the *levada* as we stroll along the path, crossing a stream which is bridged over the small channel (Wp.10 5M) before we pass a waterfall tumbling down a cleft (Wp.11 8M). Plant growth in this pocket is spectacular, with fennel bursting forth from sloping carpets of wild flowers.

The waterfall at Wp.11

While walking through the magnificent flora, it is easy to miss the end of the small *levada* channel, until our path starts to climb (Wp.12 11M) and we cross a succession of small streams before the path widens to come below a cliff face (Wp.13 24M). Shortly, darker laurels replace the tree heathers lining the path, which presage our arrival at a path junction (Wp.14 29M); our Walk 30 Bica da Cana (west) route goes north-west from this junction.

... up the sloping meadows ...

Turning up the path on our left, we face a steep climb up through zigzags and a boulder stair before the gradient eases to bring us up to a stile (Wp.15 36M). Over the stile, we still face an energetic walk up the sloping meadows, the tree heather forest restrained behind a fence on our left before we come onto the road by the 'official' entrance to **Bica da Cana** (Wp.16 43M) and its 'Miradouro' sign.

An easy couple of minutes along the tarmac brings us back to our starting point.

No *levada* this time, but a wild woodland path running below the escarpment, to meet an abandoned road project above the oft-heard of but seldom seen **Casa Caramujo**. An energetic ascent takes us up to the woodland setting of the **Estanquinhos Posto Florestal** forest house before returning across the high meadows to our start point. This route offers a rewarding, vertigo-free circuit of three contrasting landscapes.

Access by car:
No bus access but plenty of roadside parking alongside the ER110 for car drivers.

Lathyrus latifolius thrives here

We park alongside the road at the 'official' entrance to **Bica da Cana** with its 'miradouro' sign. From the corner (Wp.1 0M) we head down the path's springy turf alongside the fenced tree heather, to cross the stile before tackling the steep 'boulder stair' descent to the T-junction of paths (Wp.2 9M), where Walk 29 Bica da Cana (east) arrives from the right.

This time we go left, towards **Casa Caramujo**, our path descending steadily beneath dark cliffs which define the plateau's edge, an abundance of wild plants flourishing at the base of the wet rock. Tree heather protects our narrow path from the drops on our right, as we pass little waterfalls which tumble down the cliffs, to create streams dropping down into the valley.

Lush plant life en route

Miradouro views at 24 minutes

Plants push in on sections of our route as the cliffs seem to diminish, and the tree heather gives way for us to come on to red rock, where we enjoy *miradouro* views out over the valley (Wp.3 24M). We drop down amongst the trees, sections of the path becoming

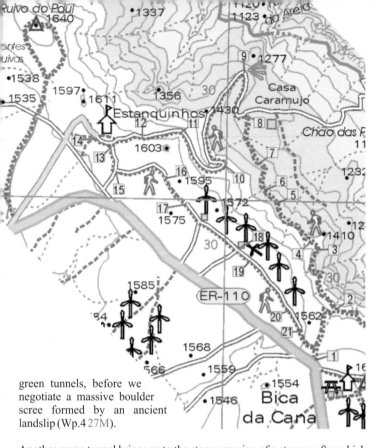

green tunnels, before we
negotiate a massive boulder
scree formed by an ancient
landslip (Wp.4 27M).

Another green tunnel brings us to the stony crossing of a stream, after which
the path becomes more open, descending through a rock channel (Wp.5 33M)
before we need to hurdle an old fallen tree.Our path is taking us steadily
downhill, an indicator of the ascents to come, as we cross another stream
(Wp.6 40M) to come onto a boulder-laid section of the route. After the laid
section we come back onto a dirt and rock surface, as we step over another
fallen tree (Wp.7 45M).

Now the forest opens up as we come to cross another stream, then climbing up
onto the dirt road above **Casa Caramujo** (Wp.8 51M 1282 metres altitude).

The open aspect of the dirt road contrasts directly with the forest environment
we have just experienced. Originally planned as a road from **Ginjas** up to the
Paúl da Serra plateau, but never completed, some maps confusingly show
this as the original proposal for a tarmac driving route. On our right, the dirt
road drops down past **Casa Caramujo** in a long, twisty descent to meet the
tarmac above **Ginjas** - an alternative route, although you will be a long way
from your car.

Now we start paying for all that downhill through the forest, as we head up the
dirt road, its much-eroded surface suitable for only the toughest of off-road
vehicles. We face a relentless ascent past the yellow broom and tree heather

which line the road, taking advantage of the *miradouro* hairpin bends (Wp.9 60M, Wp.10 86M, Wp.11 100M and Wp.12 107M) at which we can recover while enjoying the extensive views.

The shady Estanquinhos Posto Florestal

Eventually, we come up through a cutting to reach the crest of our route (Wp.13 112M) beside a 'Prohibido Faso Lume' sign. After that three hundred-plus metre ascent we stroll along to the end of the dirt road and take a break at the shady picnic area below the forest house of **Estanquinhos** (Wp.14 116M).

After the interesting woodland path, and then the stupendous views on the climb to **Estanquinhos**, our return to our start point takes us through another completely different landscape.

From below the forest house (0M), we retrace our steps along the dirt road until, before its crest, we go right on a green lane which runs gently downhill between pine trees. As we emerge from the pines, we go left (Wp.15) towards the wind turbines, climbing gently to a cross-roads (Wp.16 10M), where we go right to start closing with the turbines. We keep right at a faint junction, our route narrowing to a walking trail before we come onto an eroded dirt road (Wp.17).

Strolling beneath the turbines

The **Paúl da Serra** rolls away on our right, as we stroll past a dirt road off to our right and the wind farm control building. The huge turbines dwarf us tiny humans, and we pass a second dirt road and control building (Wp.18 21M) before pausing to examine the strangely moving sight of a dead turbine, like a huge shattered insect sprawled across the grass (Wp.19).

The road, now badly eroded, brings us past the last two turbines and another control building, and the **Bica da Cana** forest house comes into sight ahead from the last turbine (Wp.20 30M).

We stroll to the end of the green road (Wp.21) to continue on a footpath that picks its way, through rocks and then across the meadow, to meet our outward route just below the road. In a few steps, we are back at our start point.

This beautiful forest walk takes in the **Risco** waterfall and its easy strolling *levada*, though the descent/ascent from, and to, the forest house provides a small exertion. GPS reception will depend upon the location of the satellites in relation to the steep valley walls when you are walking, varying between average and poor reception.

Access by car:

It is no longer possible to drive down to **Rabaçal Posto Florestal**. Park on the grass at the top of the access road and walk down it to begin at the forest house. There may be the option of a shuttle mini-bus on the access road (€2 one way) or there's the interesting option of using the **Rabaçal - Calheta Tunnel**; see page 153 for access details. (Times and distances do not include the walk to and from the forest house.)

Extension
For a longer walk with only a little more in the way of descents and ascents join Walk 32, Levada das 25 Fontes, at the junction at Wp.3.

After walking down the access road, we pass behind the forest house to find a stone-laid path (Wp.1 0M) which leads us down from the picnic tables and toilet area. Dropping down through the shade of mature trees, we come onto the broad *levada* path to go right, curving around below the forest house.

It's easy strolling beneath magnificent trees beside the water channel, hurdling a fallen tree (Wp.2) just before we pass stone steps which lead back up to the house, followed by a

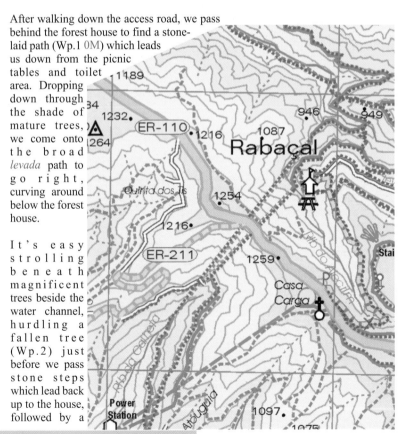

dirt road that has run down from the tarmac access road; our path widens to vehicle width until Wp.5.

We bowl along to pass a junction (Wp.3 11M) where a path is signed downhill to 'Levada das 25 Fontes'; see Walk 32 for the description of this route which can be completed as an extension of this one.

Continuing past the junction, we pass two streams feeding the *levada* at a water run-off (Wp.4 17M), and a second water run-off before passing a dirt road which drops down to the left (Wp.5 23M). Walking along the *levada* wall as it curves into the bowl at the head of the gorge, water drops onto the route giving you quite a soaking in wet weather.

The Risco waterfall

On reaching a viewing point (Wp.6 27M), we find ourselves in the midpoint of the hundred metre waterfall of **Risco**, as it plunges down into the pool below us. Take your time enjoying the scale of the landscape before returning to **Rabaçal Posto Florestal**, using either the dirt road or the stone steps.

The **25 Fontes** below **Pico Balcões** has long been a favourite walking route, despite the vertiginous nature of the *levada*. In 2003 a member of a guided walking group was killed in a freak accident, and the *levada* path was closed by the rangers. The walker wanted to send a photo on her mobile phone, but while stretching her arm out to hold the phone in front of her, she pressed back against the safety wire, which collapsed. Be warned! Although the onward route beyond our walk description was open at the time of writing and some stretches have had new steel posts and wires installed, there are still several narrow unprotected vertical drops, not recommended for vertigo sufferers. Our **25 Fontes** Tour is a gentle circular stroll along the easy part of the *levada* to the **Calheta** tunnel and back to the **Rabaçal Posto Florestal** forest house, with just the steep descent to the levada and equally steep ascent back to the forest house to disturb the tranquil atmosphere.

Access by car:
See Walk 31 for access details.

* when completing the whole route

From the end of **Rabaçal**'s tarmac access road (0M), we take the dirt road downhill, stepping over or round the chain vehicle barrier, to the **Levada do Risco** (Wp.1 3M). Turning right, we stroll along the broad vehicle-width *levada* path and come to a junction (Wp.2), where we take the downhill path signed to 'Levada das 25 Fontes'. Our stone-laid path drops steadily as a staired descent through the tree-covered side of the valley, before levelling out to contour around the valley wall as a rock and dirt path, then descending again on a stone-laid slope. A section of rock and dirt surface (Wp.3 15M) is followed by stone steps which take us down to a T-junction on the path beside the **Levada das 25 Fontes** (Wp.4 22M).

For the Adventurous
Going right we follow the traditional **25 Fontes** route through the wooded slopes, the dirt path finishing as we come onto the *levada* wall to walk suspended above the gorge for us to cross the **Ribeira Grande** on a bridge (31M). After the bridge we leave the *levada* on steps before rejoining it at a water house; where the path narrows vertiginously we have the benefit of a thigh-high parapet for support. Rampant vegetation protects us from the vertiginous drop, passing a path down to a lower *levada* (53M), as we come around to the amphitheatre filled with cascading streams dropping into pools (64M). Return the same way or you might take the zigzag path down to the **Levada da Rocha Vermelha**; an adventure in itself. Going left, we cross the **Ribeira Grande** and then left up a steep stepped path to return to the **Levada das 25 Fontes**.

Safety First Option
We retrace our steps back to the point where our path came down onto the *levada* (Wp.4 36M), to stroll westwards (W) on the broad woodland path, crossing the occasional water runoff built across the path. We come to a concrete box 'seat' (Wp.6 40M) just past an elevated concrete section of the

path, revealing large water pipes running underground alongside the original **25 Fontes** levada; the 'seat' is actually an access point to the pipeline. In another couple of minutes (Wp.7 42M) we meet the stone laid path which climbs up from the **Levada da Rocha Vermelha** from our 'adventurous route' option.

Just past the **Rocha Vermelha** path, stone and earth steps climb up to our left (Wp.8), as we continue to stroll beside the fast running water. At a cleft, the hidden pipeline short cuts the cleft (Wp.9 47M), disappearing again before we pass through a rock cutting (Wp.10) equipped with a concrete box 'seat', shortly before reaching stone steps which climb up from the *levada* towards **Rabaçal** (Wp.11 50M). This is our return route to the forest house, but before tackling the ascent, we continue beside the water channel, to the impressive setting at the entrance to the **Calheta** tunnel (Wp.12 55M).

All our route, with the possible exception of the descent to the **Levada das 25 Fontes**, has been a pleasant woodland stroll through mature forest, with views across the **Janela** valley, but this spot is the jewel of our walk. Water boils down a channel to feed the *levada*, above seating at the tunnel entrance - and what a tunnel; no need to crouch down for this one!

The channel near Calheta tunnel

A picturesque valley contains this memorable setting, making it an idyllic picnic spot. When we can tear ourselves away, we go back to the broad stone stairway (Wp.11), to commence the climb back up to the forest house. It's an energetic ascent to **Rabaçal Posto Florestal** on the oversized stone steps, as we zigzag up the near-vertical tree-covered slopes, ducking under a fallen tree (Wp.13). Ducking under more fallen and horizontally growing trees, we reach the **Levada do Risco**. We choose between going right or left on the comfortably flat *levada* path; right takes us to the stairway we used as the descent on Walk 31, a relatively short climb taking us up to the terraces at the forest house (Wp.14). The left choice gives us a longer stroll, picking up our outward route for a gentler ascent up the dirt road to the tarmac access road just above the forest house.

33 RABAÇAL: LEVADA DA RIBEIRA GRANDE

At the top of the **Rabaçal** access road is a new *levada* (at least in Madeiran terms), which feeds water into the holding tank for the **Calheta** power station alongside the main ER-110 road. We head out to a beautiful river setting, taking in an impressive water stair along the way. It's an easy walk, though it does have vertiginous sections, on this officially unnamed *levada* (but christened **Levada da Ribeira Grande** by John & Pat Underwood, famous for their 'Landscapes of Madeira' guidebook). Add in reasonably good GPS reception, and this is just the route to top out your **Rabaçal** experience.

| 1 | 2H | 7 km | ⋀⋁ | 20m / 20m | ⟷ | 2 | 🍴 0 |

Access by car:
Turn off the main ER-110 road onto the **Rabaçal** access road and park on the grass below the junction.

We park on the grass pasture near the top of the access road for **Rabaçal** (Wp.1 0M) and walk across to an electricity pylon (Wp.2) which marks the start of a path running up to the *levada* (Wp.3 2M). A comfortable dirt path framed by tree heather runs alongside this modern *levada*, the heather unfortunately obscuring most of the views, though the ease of the path goes some way to compensate for this.

Heading off against the water flow, we pass occasional slabs bridging the channel, one of which leads to a weather station (Wp.4 10M). Past a short, unprotected drop (Wp.5 11M), we come to a water collection pool teeming with trout (Wp.6 13M) beside the **Ribeira do Alecrím** whose waters are diverted into the pool.

Across the river, our easy path continues past a spring (Wp.7) before coming to a viewpoint (Wp.8 18M) which overlooks our start point. At a pair of rock cuttings (Wp.9 20M, and slightly vertiginous) you might choose to walk in the water channel, but this minor hazard is soon forgotten as we come to a spectacular water stair (Wp.10 25M). Water charges down the steep channel, as

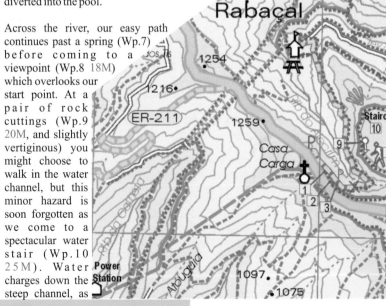

… a spectacular water stair …

we ascend on a stone slab stair - far less vertiginous than it looks - to a *miradouro* viewpoint at the head of the stair.

The *levada* above the stair narrows noticeably, as we curve towards the **Ribeira Grande**, crossing a short vertiginous section (Wp.11) before the easy walking continues. If you're extremely observant along this section, you may spot the junction with our Walk 34, Blue Hat Ascent (Wp.12); if you're lucky enough to see walkers emerging from this route it's a memorable sight - almost as if they are growing out of the ground, their inevitable coating of mud supporting this illusion.

We continue, our path made slightly vertiginous as we reach a section where tiny channels and streams feed the *levada* (Wp.13 43M), and five minutes later careful footwork is required to cross a water runoff (Wp.14 48M). Past a pleasant pool and waterfall (Wp.15), we come under a wet cliff face, just before reaching the source of the *levada* at **Ribeira Grande** (Wp.16 53M).

A concrete barrage has been built across the watercourse to ensure a constant water flow into the *levada*, though storm waters charge over this barrier. The result is a beautiful pool which, together with this river valley setting, make this one of Madeira's best locations for a picnic.

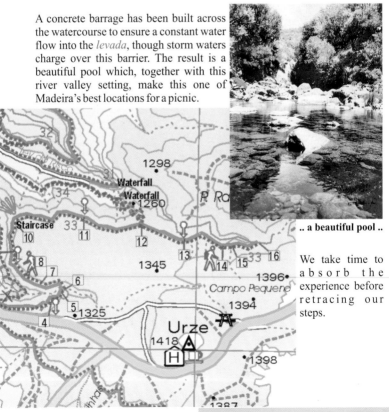

.. a beautiful pool ..

We take time to absorb the experience before retracing our steps.

The *levadas* of **Rabaçal** are well known, and from deep in the bowl at the head of the **Janela Gorge** the steep forested slopes in this area look impenetrable. You might think that the narrow access road is the only way in and out - not so. Here is a little-known route that climbs up from **Rabaçal Posto Florestal** to emerge onto the **Levada da Ribeira Grande**.

Not for the faint hearted; it's a slippery ascent, even in the driest of weather, so don't even consider this route in wet weather. An energetic two hundred metre ascent with negligible views brings us to the *levada*, yet there's a great sense of achievement when completed. There's poor GPS reception in the forest and a high chance of getting very muddy during the ascent.

Access by car:
Turn off the main ER-110 road onto the **Rabaçal** access road and park on the grass below the junction.

Short walk alternative
Follow the main route to the path junction at 58 minutes. Go straight ahead at the junction to a relatively open section of forest with waterfalls. Return the same way (2 hours).

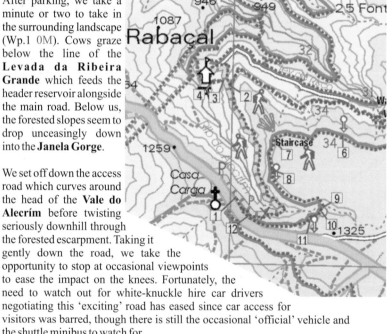

After parking, we take a minute or two to take in the surrounding landscape (Wp.1 0M). Cows graze below the line of the **Levada da Ribeira Grande** which feeds the header reservoir alongside the main road. Below us, the forested slopes seem to drop unceasingly down into the **Janela Gorge**.

We set off down the access road which curves around the head of the **Vale do Alecrím** before twisting seriously downhill through the forested escarpment. Taking it gently down the road, we take the opportunity to stop at occasional viewpoints to ease the impact on the knees. Fortunately, the need to watch out for white-knuckle hire car drivers negotiating this 'exciting' road has eased since car access for visitors was barred, though there is still the occasional 'official' vehicle and the shuttle minibus to watch for.

Twenty minutes down the road, depending on your walking pace, sees us at the point where our walking trail crosses the road (Wp.2 20M); though you are more likely to miss this almost hidden path. You can short cut onto the

ascent at this point, though normally you would continue down past the upward path (Wp.3 and easier to see) to the end of the tarmac and walking over to the forest house of **Rabaçal** (25M); if only there was a café here.
When you've enjoyed this spectacular setting we can head off on our 'Blue Hat' ascent.

Passing from the front of the house to its rear terraces, there is a crudely cut, narrow stone stair cut into the rock on the left; this insignificant path (insignificant in **Rabaçal** terms) is the start of our route back to the top (0M) The stair climbs up to pass the end of the car parking area (Wp.4), after which the rough path climbs steeply up to meet the access road (Wp.3 8M). Up the road for a few metres, and we find our trail's continuation (Wp.2) which climbs steeply up from the tarmac and into the trees; poor to very poor GPS coverage.

Dense vegetation on this wet route

The gradient eases as our narrow path meanders along through the forest, many of the trees growing out almost horizontally. Sounds of waterfalls drift up to us, and streams cross our trail, creating wet areas needing careful footwork.

We are walking above - almost vertically above - the **Levada do Risco** path, but how different this forest trail is to the relaxed stroll down below.

After the third stream crossing, our trail starts climbing (25M) on a stony surface which incorporates stone and tree root steps.

There are more stream crossings requiring careful footwork, before the path narrows (again, choose your steps carefully) and still climbs steadily to come to a path junction (58M).

If we go ahead, in two minutes the path leads to an open section of the forest with pleasant waterfalls, a suitable short walk alternative. Going right at the junction, we are into some serious forest climbing, arms doing as much work as legs at times. If in doubt, look upwards to confirm the way ahead. Streams abound, fed by springs from below **Pico da Urze** and you will be doing very well if you can reach the top of the climb without becoming mud covered by at least one stream crossing.

In this dense forest, GPS reception is almost non-existent, and the same applies to the views. This is a relentless ascent, so rest when you need to; we do, eventually, clamber up into the open alongside the welcomingly bright and airy *levada* (Wp.5 94M).

Blue echium thrives in this section

After that sombre, muddy forest, the *levada* path seems like heaven. We go right, but don't relax too much as we need to negotiate a short vertiginous section (Wp.6 99M) before strolling along to the head of a remarkable water staircase (Wp.7 108M) with *miradouro* views. The slab step descent alongside the racing water needs concentration, but is not as vertiginous as it first looks.

Our route continues, lined by lush vegetation, encountering two vertiginous cuttings (Wp.8 112M) before we reach a large water collection pool teeming with fish (Wp.9 120M).

Just past the fish is a narrow vertiginous section of concrete (Wp.10 122M), after which we can relax into an easy stroll, passing a weather station on our left (Wp.11). Shortly after, we step off the *levada* (Wp.12 131M) onto the green pastures at the top of the access road for **Rabaçal**. A dirt path takes us over the meadows and back to our car (Wp.1 135M).

The **Janela Gorge** is most impressive, both at its head around **Rabaçal** and here at its mouth, where we enjoy unforgettable views over the great valley on almost every step of our route. You'll soon appreciate why we've named this 'The Garden Levada', as it seems as if Groundforce must have been through the first half of our route, siting picnic tables and rustic railings at the best *miradouro* viewpoints alongside the canal. In the second half the *levada* is more rugged, with safety wires protecting us from drops - a head for heights will certainly help. (GPS reception is poor on the final section of the outward route.)

Access by bus:

Bus riders should alight at **Porto Moniz** and take a taxi to **Levada Ribeira da Janela**; your downhill walking return from **Lamaceiros** back to **Porto Moniz** will give you a second memorable route.

> **Short Walk**
> Follow the main route to the picnic spot at Wp.8 and return (50 minutes).

Access by car:

Leave **Porto Moniz** on the ER-101 for the zigzag climb up the escarpment before turning left towards **Lamaceiros** (signed). Continue through the village, and follow the signs to the *levada*, to park near the large circular header tank feeding **Ribeira da Janela**'s little power station.

The start of the route

If full, park alongside the 'main' road where there is plenty of parking both before and beyond the point where you cross the *levada*.

We start out from the picnic tables (Wp.1 0M) on the broad agapanthus-lined grassy path which curves right past another picnic table before crossing the road (more parking) to head up the valley, the route accompanied by street lighting.

Just past a nicely situated picnic table (Wp.2), a concrete walkway with railings takes us past a filtration section of the *levada* (Wp.3 4M).

The picnic table at Wp.2

Our broad path, still lined with agapanthus, gives us views up the mighty valley to **Paúl da Serra**. Passing a section of path protected by wooden railings, and a water runoff bridged over the *levada* which also has wooden railings, we come to the best sited of the picnic tables (Wp.4 12M); if it's free, grab it and have your picnic while drinking in these wonderful views.

We pass through an area of soaring eucalyptus trees, the agapanthus alongside our path now interspersed with hydrangea, before we come under darker laurel trees and to a picnic table sited in the woods (Wp.5 16M).

Agapanthus thrive on the route

After a section of path protected by railings we emerge from the woods to views to the **Paúl da Serra** (Wp.6), the route reverting to its airy nature after the shadowy laurel woodland.

Over a paved section of the *levada*, we're again walking on a dirt path surface before crossing a flood-off section with triangular stepping stones, and a narrow concrete *levada* path protected by railings (Wp.7 22M) which brings us to one of the prettiest spots on the route.

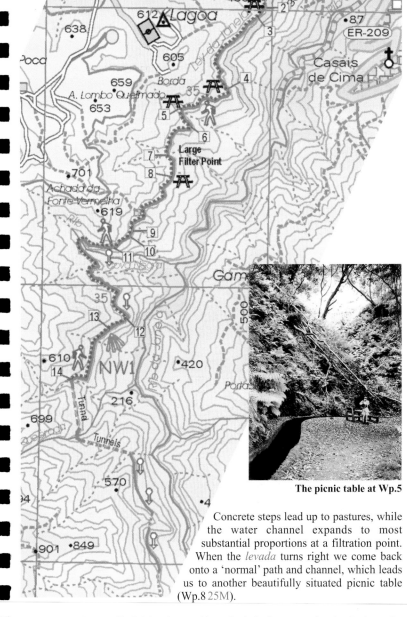

The picnic table at Wp.5

Concrete steps lead up to pastures, while the water channel expands to most substantial proportions at a filtration point. When the *levada* turns right we come back onto a 'normal' path and channel, which leads us to another beautifully situated picnic table (Wp.8 25M).

Our short walk finishes here with a picnic before returning back along the *levada*; one of Madeira's most beautiful strolls.

Beyond the picnic table our route begins to take on a darker nature; now more sections are protected by railings (not always necessary), and we come into laurel forest shading the water channel. Worth noting are the remains of two engines and *teleféricos* beside the water channel (Wps.9 & 10) which bear witness to the time when supplies were ferried up from the valley during the construction of the *levada*.

A section of our route runs below a cliff (Wp.11 35M) with an unprotected drop - this stretch might disturb vertigo sufferers - which presages further narrow sections of path protected by railings as we go into a cleft in the valley wall, to cross the slippery water runoff of the **Ribeira da Cova Negra**. Water showers down on the route as it heads back towards the main valley, and then the *levada* runs into a series of wet clefts in the valley wall, one of which contains fine examples of ferns colonising the fissure (45M).

Emerging from the trees, we enjoy fine views up the **Janela Valley** (Wp.12 52M); there is another notable viewpoint on a broader section protected by wooden railings (Wp.13) before we turn into our final cleft with narrow path and railings, where we come to our finish at the first of the *levada* tunnels across from the cleft's water runoff (Wp.14 60M).

We retrace our steps to return to **Lamaceiros** with fine views over the village and north-west coast as we approach our start point.

Views to Lamaceiros village on our return

Extension (for experts only)
Beyond this point there is a series of tunnels and an extremely vertiginous *levada*, which comes to a *levadeiros'* house. Here, a steep path/track climbs up to **Fonte do Bispo**; not recommended except for wet route experts only.

The **Fanal** region, with its grazing pastures and forest house, used to be one of Madeira's least accessible areas. To reach **Fanal** meant a truly awful nine kilometre drive along an eroded dirt road, from the ER-110 on **Paúl da Serra**. How quickly things have changed - an extension of the ER-209 has been surfaced up to the **Fanal Posto Florestal**, while that terrible dirt road has been replaced by a modern tarmac road, making this region comfortably accessible. Not that there's much at **Fanal**, beyond a basic picnic area, but there's tranquility and a gentle, natural beauty. Escape the crowds and return to nature on our two simple **Fanal** strolls.

Access by car:
For both routes, drive to **Fanal** on the ER-209 and park near the forest house or picnic area.

At the start of the western route

FANAL WEST

This simple half-hour stroll takes in views over the north coast.

2 | (¾H) | 1.5 km | 40m / 40m | 0 | 0

From the parking area before the forest house (Wp.1 0M), we go past the vehicle barrier and house to swing left on a broad grassy track, passing a camping area on our left.

Past an old water trough (Wp.2), we head towards a tree-covered knoll and reach a *miradouro* viewpoint on our right at the edge of the escarpment (Wp.3), overlooking the dramatic **Funda Valley**.

Overlooking the Funda Valley

Back on our green track, we then leave it as it swings left towards the ER-209, to go through a fence gateway (Wp.4) and begin to climb a knoll. As we approach its top the views through the trees open up, and keeping just back from its north face, we follow the line of the knoll until it starts to step downhill (Wp.5 16M).

As we return to the forest house, we have the choice of climbing the grassy peaks to the north, for further impressive views down into the **Funda Valley**.

FANAL EAST

We have an easy circular stroll, though the return section is now part of the new tarmac road which is replacing the old cobbled trail.

We start out by climbing the steps just before the forest house (Wp.6 0M, following concrete and then grass steps to an aerial, and then up to twin flagpoles (Wp.7); from here, we enjoy views across **Fanal** to the **Paúl da Serra**. We come over the crest and then meet a dirt road at the end of a tarmac spur off the forest house road (Wp.8).

Ancient laurels at Fanal

Following the dirt road, with the green hump of **Pedreira** on our left, we pass a green hut and come to a junction of green roads (Wp.9 10M) in the centre of a meadow. We go straight on across a cross roads of green roads (Wp.10) to start climbing gently between tree heathers.

Once over the crest of the road, we have an easy saunter downhill through a cutting, before we pass minor tracks off to the right and left. Our green lane comes to an abrupt end at a small earth bank; these tracks are used for harvesting the tree heather, rather than acting as access ways.

Fine views at the short diversion

Over the earth bank, we are in a channel, and take a short diversion to the left which brings us to views overlooking the valley. We return, to cross through low heathers, reaching what was once a cobbled track, now being turned into a modern tarmac road (Wp.11 30M) on which we complete our circuit, easy but sadly not as 'countrified' as the track it replaces.

After passing a new *miradouro* with views over the **Janela Valley** (Wp.12 43M), we continue along the road until we turn right into our forest house starting point (Wp.6 56M).

See our notes on GPS use and waypoints in the Introduction. All waypoints are quoted for the WGS84 datum in degrees and minutes of Latitude and Longitude.

1

WESTERN FUNCHAL GRAND TOUR

Wp	N	W
1	32 38.6274	16 55.7142
2	32 38.6052	16 55.7808
3	32 38.5782	16 55.8360
4	32 38.4420	16 55.9626
5	32 38.4390	16 56.0760
6	32 38.4150	16 56.2356
7	32 38.4360	16 56.5236
8	32 38.5716	16 56.6256
9	32 38.6274	16 56.6532
10	32 38.7318	16 56.7354
11	32 38.7846	16 56.8776
12	32 38.7198	16 56.9928
13	32 38.6982	16 57.1842
14	32 38.6898	16 57.2592
15	32 38.8206	16 57.5520
16	32 38.8398	16 57.4758
17	32 38.9460	16 57.4932
18	32 38.9886	16 57.4530
19	32 39.0234	16 57.5364
20	32 39.0348	16 57.5178
21	32 39.0474	16 57.5838
22	32 39.3330	16 57.5550
23	32 39.2292	16 57.7278
24	32 39.5106	16 57.6420
25	32 39.6312	16 57.5790
26	32 39.6642	16 57.4566
27	32 39.6246	16 57.4134
28	32 39.4356	16 57.3204
29	32 39.5232	16 57.1452
30	32 39.5112	16 57.0966
31	32 39.3840	16 56.9544
32	32 39.3156	16 56.9610
33	32 39.2982	16 56.9460
34	32 39.3030	16 56.8128
35	32 39.2538	16 56.4924
36	32 39.2154	16 56.5086
37	32 39.2250	16 56.4600
38	32 39.1104	16 56.2260
39	32 39.0012	16 56.1318
40	32 38.8536	16 56.1006
41	32 38.7672	16 55.9860
42	32 38.6784	16 55.9746
43	32 38.5578	16 56.0310
44	32 38.6094	16 55.7760
45	32 38.4924	16 55.7064
46	32 38.2962	16 55.8366

2

TERREIRO DA LUTA - BODY AND SOUL

Wp	N	W
1	32 40.5930	16 54.1976
2	32 40.6296	16 54.1224
3	32 40.7454	16 54.0510
4	32 40.7844	16 54.0444
5	32 40.7940	16 54.0468
6	32 40.8432	16 54.0660
7	32 40.8936	16 54.0660
8	32 40.9404	16 54.0258
9	32 40.9476	16 54.0042
10	32 40.9872	16 53.9646
11	32 41.0268	16 53.9682
12	32 41.0532	16 53.9730
13	32 41.0580	16 54.0036
14	32 41.1084	16 54.0228
15	32 41.1054	16 54.0114
16	32 41.0550	16 53.9310
17	32 40.7154	16 54.0582
18	32 40.7082	16 54.0834
19	32 40.6812	16 54.0702

3

BOM SUCESSO - THE ROUTE TO TOWN

Wp	N	W
1	32 40.5624	16 53.9688
2	32 40.6830	16 53.7576
3	32 40.7508	16 53.6382
4	32 40.6632	16 53.5944
5	32 40.5822	16 53.6988
6	32 40.5750	16 53.7258
7	32 40.5276	16 53.6910
8	32 40.4472	16 53.7246
9	32 40.4124	16 53.6976
10	32 40.2738	16 53.7102
11	32 40.1868	16 53.7108
12	32 40.1694	16 53.7396
13	32 40.1550	16 53.7276
14	32 40.1478	16 53.7228
15	32 39.9924	16 53.8182
16	32 39.9402	16 53.7678
17	32 39.7260	16 53.8398
18	32 39.5286	16 53.9232
19	32 39.4278	16 53.9328
20	32 39.3846	16 54.0246
21	32 38.8824	16 54.2724

4

CURRAL ROMEIROS - BABOSAS/MONTE
(Traditional Route)

Wp	N	W
1	32 40.5312	16 53.4942
2	32 40.6674	16 53.6028
3	32 40.7550	16 53.6412
4	32 40.6794	16 53.7600
5	32 40.5882	16 53.9424
6	32 40.5408	16 54.0150
7	32 40.5234	16 54.1566
8	32 40.5960	16 54.1974

5

NEW LEVADA DOS TORNOS: BABOSAS/MONTE - CURRAL ROMEIROS

Wp	N	W
1	32 40.5960	16 54.1974
2	32 40.5888	16 53.9460
3	32 40.6794	16 53.7600
4	32 40.9747	16 53.7145
5	32 41.0103	16 53.6544

6

TEA & SCONES: ROMEIROS - JASMIN TEA HOUSE

Wp	N	W
1	32 40.5654	16 53.4102
2	32 40.3506	16 53.3634
3	32 40.3152	16 53.3946
4	32 40.2318	16 53.3010
5	32 40.2858	16 53.2194
6	32 40.2192	16 53.1864
7	32 40.1058	16 53.0904
8	32 40.0746	16 53.0754
9	32 40.1448	16 52.8846
10	32 40.0458	16 52.8498
11	32 39.9690	16 52.6878
12	32 39.9846	16 52.5204
13	32 39.9492	16 52.4346

7

JASMIN TEA HOUSE - CAMACHA CENTRE

Wp	N	W
1	32 39.9492	16 52.4346
2	32 39.8676	16 52.0854
3	32 39.8586	16 51.9294
4	32 40.0392	16 51.9426
5	32 40.0080	16 51.7068

6	32	39.9036	16 51.6450
7	32	39.9780	16 51.5286
8	32	39.9408	16 51.4824
9	32	40.0014	16 51.4764
10	32	40.0074	16 51.4458
11	32	39.9000	16 51.1278
12	32	40.0146	16 51.1608
13	32	40.1736	16 51.1638
14	32	40.1166	16 51.0702
15	32	40.1802	16 51.0210
16	32	40.2390	16 50.9352
17	32	40.3056	16 50.9202
18	32	40.3302	16 50.9634
19	32	40.5090	16 50.7594
20	32	40.4322	16 50.5962
21	32	40.4466	16 50.5158
22	32	40.6074	16 50.5326
23	32	40.6500	16 50.3808
24	32	40.7778	16 50.6556

8
CAMACHA (shopping) - LEVADA DA SERRA WEST - BAR MIRANDA

Wp		N	W
1	32	40.5768	16 51.1290
2	32	40.5420	16 51.3390
3	32	40.6560	16 51.2484
4	32	40.6728	16 51.4098
5	32	40.7610	16 51.6714
6	32	40.6776	16 51.8226
7	32	40.7088	16 51.8952
8	32	40.5156	16 51.8028
9	32	40.3662	16 51.8070
10	32	40.4322	16 52.1346
11	32	40.3290	16 52.1898
12	32	40.2534	16 52.4904
13	32	40.4604	16 52.8084
14	32	40.4778	16 52.8186
15	32	40.3740	16 52.9656
16	32	40.2192	16 53.1870
17	32	40.0794	16 53.3406
18	32	39.9906	16 53.3994

9
CAMACHA - LEVADA DA SERRA EAST - CAMACHA

Wp		N	W
1	32	40.5804	16 51.1272
2	32	40.5930	16 51.1854
3	32	40.6548	16 51.2460
4	32	40.9578	16 51.2400
5	32	41.1000	16 51.3108
6	32	41.1378	16 51.1866
7	32	41.2590	16 51.4242
8	32	41.3052	16 51.1542
9	32	41.2404	16 51.0114
10	32	41.1426	16 51.1032
11	32	41.0934	16 50.9790
12	32	41.0016	16 50.8698
13	32	40.9062	16 50.7648
14	32	40.8264	16 50.7504

10
LEVADA DO CANIÇO

Wp		N	W
1	32	40.7610	16 50.5980
2	32	40.7526	16 50.4690
3	32	40.6494	16 50.3808
4	32	40.6332	16 50.3748
5	32	40.7130	16 50.3364
6	32	40.7610	16 50.2896
7	32	40.7304	16 50.1882
8	32	40.6014	16 50.0418
9	32	40.5390	16 50.0628
10	32	40.4238	16 50.1726
11	32	40.2828	16 49.9818
12	32	40.2600	16 50.0190
13	32	40.2204	16 50.1390
14	32	40.1532	16 49.8828
15	32	40.0356	16 49.7076
16	32	39.9012	16 49.5720
17	32	39.8376	16 49.5918
18	32	39.7542	16 49.4940
19	32	39.6018	16 49.4628
20	32	39.5730	16 49.5492
21	32	39.5562	16 49.5870

11
BALCÕES

Wp		N	W
1	32	44.1306	16 53.1732
2	32	44.1774	16 53.2914
3	32	44.2272	16 53.2698
4	32	44.3442	16 53.3136
5	32	44.4618	16 53.3070
6	32	44.4702	16 53.3550
7	32	44.4948	16 53.4180
8	32	44.2596	16 53.5109

12
RIBEIRO FRIO CIRCULAR TOUR

Wp		N	W
1	32	44.1036	16 53.1792
2	32	44.3226	16 52.8516
3	32	44.3286	16 52.7874
4	32	44.3034	16 52.7394
5	32	44.2908	16 52.7196
6	32	44.2332	16 52.5954
7	32	44.2122	16 52.1994
8	32	44.0364	16 52.2414
9	32	43.9764	16 52.3596
10	32	43.9476	16 52.5936
11	32	43.8666	16 52.6434
12	32	43.7652	16 52.8210
13	32	43.7274	16 52.8126
14	32	43.7280	16 52.8648
15	32	43.7076	16 52.9140
16	32	43.6434	16 52.9602
17	32	43.6440	16 53.0004
18	32	43.6380	16 53.0790
19	32	43.8306	16 53.0802
20	32	43.8024	16 53.1888
21	32	43.8402	16 53.1534
22	32	43.8246	16 53.2452
23	32	43.8678	16 53.2488
24	32	43.9218	16 53.1948
25	32	44.0214	16 53.2590

13
PORTELA BOUND

Wp		N	W
1	32	44.1036	16 53.1792
2	32	44.3226	16 52.8516
3	32	44.3286	16 52.7874
4	32	44.3034	16 52.7394
5	32	44.2908	16 52.7196
6	32	44.2332	16 52.5954
7	32	44.2122	16 52.1994
8	32	44.0364	16 52.2414
9	32	44.3736	16 50.8320
10	32	44.4732	16 50.6832
11	32	44.6250	16 50.3676
12	32	44.7102	16 49.7880
13	32	44.7270	16 49.5822
14	32	44.8356	16 49.5420

14
A WIZARDLY TOWER (PICO DO SUNA)

Wp		N	W
1	32	44.8356	16 49.5420
2	32	44.7270	16 49.5822
3	32	44.7102	16 49.7880
4	32	44.7612	16 50.2194
5	32	44.6250	16 50.3676
6	32	44.5512	16 50.5236
7	32	44.4732	16 50.6832
8	32	44.2404	16 50.8830
9	32	44.3736	16 50.8314
10	32	44.3592	16 50.8542
11	32	44.2992	16 50.9316
12	32	44.2776	16 51.0096
13	32	44.2056	16 51.1992
14	32	44.1492	16 51.2316
15	32	44.1492	16 51.2388
16	32	44.2572	16 51.2256

15
PORTELA - SANTO DA SERRA

Wp		N	W
1	32	44.8356	16 49.5420
2	32	44.7270	16 49.5822
3	32	44.7102	16 49.7880
4	32	44.7612	16 50.2194

5	32	44.6250	16 50.3676
6	32	44.5512	16 50.5236
7	32	44.4732	16 50.6832
8	32	44.1948	16 50.8554
9	32	44.2362	16 50.7924
10	32	44.2206	16 50.7588
11	32	44.0094	16 50.4432
12	32	43.9944	16 50.4270
13	32	43.9674	16 50.3214
14	32	43.9404	16 50.2188
15	32	43.9242	16 50.1486
16	32	43.7772	16 49.9518
17	32	43.6668	16 49.7862
18	32	43.7184	16 49.7928
19	32	43.5816	16 49.6380
20	32	43.4586	16 49.1454

16
LEVADA DO CASTELEJO

Wp		N	W
1	32	46.0308	16 51.0486
2	32	45.9312	16 50.7936
3	32	46.0032	16 50.6970
4	32	45.9276	16 50.6976
5	32	45.8442	16 50.3940
6	32	45.8178	16 50.3466
7	32	45.6942	16 50.4558
8	32	45.5718	16 50.4402
9	32	45.5016	16 50.5830
10	32	45.3990	16 50.4468
11	32	45.3084	16 50.3934
12	32	45.3018	16 50.1348
13	32	45.2910	16 50.0274

17
THE GREEN POOL
(Caldeirão Verde - nearly)

Wp		N	W
1	32	46.7874	16 53.8092
2	32	46.7814	16 53.9118
3	32	46.9458	16 54.2010
4	32	46.8570	16 54.3906
5	32	46.8462	16 54.4320
6	32	47.0196	16 54.3480
7	32	47.0862	16 54.4092
8	32	47.1156	16 54.4350
9	32	47.1714	16 54.4986
10	32	47.0478	16 54.6810
11	32	46.9872	16 54.7584
12	32	46.9728	16 54.8190
13	32	46.8432	16 55.0212
14	32	47.0868	16 55.0338
15	32	46.9758	16 55.1694
16	32	46.7856	16 55.2624
17	32	46.7382	16 55.3098

18
PICO DO RUIVO

Wp		N	W
1	32	45.8904	16 55.2660
2	32	45.8820	16 55.5126
3	32	45.7962	16 55.6830
4	32	45.7926	16 55.9458
5	32	45.6726	16 56.1378
6	32	45.6654	16 56.2044
7	32	45.6318	16 56.3466
8	32	45.6090	16 56.4606
9	32	45.6186	16 56.4912
10	32	45.6090	16 56.6010
11	32	45.5268	16 56.5572

PICO DO ARIERO (notes)

Wp		N	W
1	32	44.1132	16 55.7280
2	32	44.1264	16 55.7232
3	32	44.2008	16 55.9038
4	32	44.2554	16 55.9524
5	32	44.3526	16 56.0172

19
SÃO LOURENÇO PENINSULA

Wp	N	W
1	32	44.6028 16 42.0546
2	32	44.6694 16 42.0414
3	32	44.8194 16 41.8836
4	32	44.8398 16 41.8584
5	32	44.9208 16 41.8506
6	32	44.9088 16 41.7684
7	32	44.9322 16 41.7726
8	32	45.0066 16 41.7450
9	32	45.0234 16 41.6952
10	32	45.0342 16 41.6664
11	32	45.0264 16 41.6436
12	32	44.9808 16 41.6220
13	32	44.9178 16 41.6046
14	32	44.9370 16 41.5254
15	32	44.7948 16 41.4366
16	32	44.7810 16 41.2560
17	32	44.6886 16 41.1714
18	32	44.6250 16 41.1876
19	32	44.5614 16 41.1498
20	32	44.5302 16 41.1666
21	32	44.5506 16 41.1012
22	32	44.4780 16 41.0394
23	32	44.5176 16 41.0052
24	32	44.5716 16 40.9104

20
LEVADA DO CANIÇAL (west)

Wp		N	W
1		unreliable reception	
2		unreliable reception	
3	32	44.3514	16 47.9592
4	32	44.3964	16 47.9226
5	32	44.3160	16 47.8638
6	32	44.2164	16 47.6046
7	32	44.3010	16 47.4888
8	32	44.4690	16 47.4588
9	32	44.1210	16 47.1072
10	32	44.1252	16 46.9674
11	32	44.5074	16 47.0892
12	32	44.7426	16 46.9560
13	32	44.5584	16 46.8906
14	32	44.5926	16 46.6812
15	32	44.9988	16 46.3944
16	32	44.7780	16 46.4034
17	32	44.5542	16 46.4166
18	32	44.5800	16 46.3140
19	32	44.2806	16 46.3668
20	32	43.9819	16 45.8588

21
PICO DO FACHO

Wp		N	W
1	32	43.9686	16 45.8472
2	32	43.5438	16 45.5688
3	32	43.4394	16 45.5070
4	32	43.4358	16 45.5538
5	32	43.5150	16 45.6318
6	32	43.5312	16 45.7080
7	32	43.4238	16 45.8508
8	32	43.1184	16 45.5550
9	32	43.1610	16 45.8670

22
LEVADA DO CANIÇAL EAST

Wp		N	W
1	32	44.2248	16 45.4554
2	32	44.2944	16 45.3324
3	32	44.3976	16 44.9022
4	32	44.5434	16 44.9886
5	32	44.7654	16 44.9466
6	32	44.8632	16 45.0090
7	32	44.8950	16 44.9352
8	32	45.0300	16 45.0438
9	32	44.9898	16 44.7228
10	32	45.0528	16 44.6538
11	32	44.5182	16 44.2560
12	32	44.2428	16 44.2998

23
OLD TRAIL TO CANIÇAL

Wp		N	W
1	32	43.9650	16 45.8544
2	32	43.5414	16 45.5700
3	32	43.7580	16 45.2640
4	32	43.8294	16 45.2922
5	32	43.8780	16 44.9874
6	32	44.0832	16 44.8254
7	32	44.1816	16 44.7948
8	32	44.1126	16 44.7336
9	32	44.1349	16 44.4066
10	32	44.2440	16 44.3022

24

BOCA DO RISCO

Wp		N		W
1	32	43.1076	16	45.9510
2	32	43.7016	16	46.1466
3	32	43.8822	16	46.2720
4	32	43.9824	16	46.4490
5	32	44.2596	16	46.5786
6	32	44.4582	16	46.4934
7	32	44.4954	16	46.4604
8	32	4.5524	16	46.4184
9	32	44.7696	16	46.4010
10	32	44.9502	16	46.3524
11	32	45.0114	16	46.2246
12	32	45.1482	16	46.1862
13	32	45.2508	16	46.2264
14	32	45.3336	16	46.3476
15	32	44.6094	16	46.4388
16	32	44.5638	16	46.5108
17	32	44.5440	16	46.4994

25

PORTELA WOODLAND CIRCULAR

Wp		N		W
1	32	44.8338	16	49.5426
2	32	44.7492	16	49.0722
3	32	44.7096	16	48.9708
4	32	44.7528	16	48.9300
5	32	44.8098	16	48.8622
6	32	44.9610	16	48.6864
7	32	45.0570	16	48.7092
8	32	45.4044	16	48.4824
9	32	45.3078	16	47.9940
10	32	45.3384	16	47.9358
11	32	45.2066	16	48.0111
12	32	44.9310	16	48.4290
13	32	44.8482	16	48.5550
14	32	44.7930	16	48.4692
15	32	44.7882	16	48.4134
16	32	44.6718	16	48.2772
17	32	44.5662	16	48.3012
18	32	44.3628	16	48.2964
19	32	44.3022	16	48.4122
20	32	44.3076	16	48.8316
21	32	44.3574	16	48.9438
22	32	44.6250	16	49.0080
23	32	44.6772	16	49.3362
24	32	44.7996	16	49.4244

26

ALL WEATHER STROLLING: MACHICO - RIBEIRA SECA

Wp		N		W
1	32	43.1076	16	45.9510
2	32	43.1610	16	45.8670
3	32	43.7016	16	46.1466
4	32	43.8822	16	46.2720
5	32	43.9824	16	46.4490
6	32	44.2188	16	46.5738
7	32	44.4576	16	46.4910
8	32	44.5632	16	46.5132
9	32	44.4132	16	46.8228
10	32	44.3364	16	46.7652
11	32	44.2482	16	46.7622
12	32	44.2200	16	46.6836
13	32	43.9938	16	46.5360
14	32	43.9428	16	46.4766

27

LEVADA DO NORTE - ENCUMEADA

Wp		N		W
1	32	45.2520	17	01.1544
2	32	45.2544	17	01.3734
3	32	45.2580	17	01.3992
4	32	45.2544	17	01.5042
5	32	45.1908	17	01.5774
6	32	45.1104	17	01.5972
7	32	45.0804	17	01.6974
8	32	45.2358	17	01.1508
9	32	45.1104	17	00.9894
10	32	45.0798	17	00.9684
11	32	45.0324	17	00.9888
12	32	45.0054	17	00.9936

28

THE GRASS BRIDGE: CURRAL JANGÃO

Wp		N		W
1	32	45.1812	17	01.2492
2	32	45.0996	17	01.0956
3	32	45.0378	17	01.0812
4	32	44.9472	17	01.0776
5	32	44.8842	17	00.9780
6	32	44.8668	17	00.8112
7	32	44.9118	17	00.5736
8	32	44.9040	17	00.3204
9	32	44.7534	16	59.9730
10	32	44.7066	16	59.8962

29

BICA DA CANA (east)

Wp		N		W
1	32	45.3650	17	03.5585
2	32	45.3876	17	03.4320
3	32	45.3738	17	03.2898
4	32	45.3654	17	03.3168
5	32	45.2568	17	03.2526
6	32	45.2682	17	03.2064
7	32	45.2778	17	03.1320
8	32	45.2298	17	03.0804
9	32	45.1926	17	03.0738
10	32	45.2904	17	03.1722
11	32	45.3390	17	03.2130
12	32	45.3756	17	03.1818
13	32	45.5766	17	03.3264
14	32	45.6246	17	03.4692
15	32	45.6096	17	03.5160
16	32	45.4518	17	03.5622

30

BICA DA CANA (west)

Wp		N		W
1	32	45.4518	17	03.5622
2	32	45.6246	17	03.4692
3	32	45.8436	17	03.5562
4	32	45.8634	17	03.5970
5	32	46.0074	17	03.7404
6	32	46.0440	17	03.7998
7	32	46.1526	17	03.8334
8	32	46.2828	17	03.8862
9	32	46.4664	17	03.8838
10	32	46.1286	17	03.9744
11	32	46.2486	17	04.1598
12	32	46.2246	17	04.3614
13	32	46.1910	17	04.4916
14	32	46.2204	17	04.5630
15	32	46.1004	17	04.4724
16	32	46.1178	17	04.2942
17	32	45.9792	17	04.1238
18	32	45.8262	17	03.9126
19	32	45.7818	17	03.8358
20	32	45.6174	17	03.6744
21	32	45.5418	17	03.6174

31

RABAÇAL - LEVADA DO RISCO

Wp		N		W
1	32	45.6984	17	08.1054
2	32	45.7188	17	08.0634
3	32	45.7368	17	07.8996
4	32	45.6564	17	07.6806
5	32	45.6366	17	07.4904
6	32	45.6090	17	07.4304

32

RABAÇAL - LEVADA DAS 25 FONTES TOUR

Wp		N		W
1	32	45.7812	17	07.9620
2	32	45.7368	17	07.8996
3	32	45.7356	17	07.8132
4	32	45.6396	17	07.6398
5	32	45.7386	17	07.6518
6	32	45.8148	17	07.8744
7	32	45.8184	17	07.8828
8	32	45.8274	17	07.8936
9	32	45.7890	17	08.0568
10	32	45.7806	17	08.1102
11	32	45.7392	17	08.1726
12	32	45.6732	17	08.1726
13	32	45.6846	17	08.1426
14	32	45.6984	17	08.1054

33 RABAÇAL - LEVADA DA RIBEIRA GRANDE

Wp	N	W
1	32 45.2628	17 07.9980
2	32 45.2352	17 07.9758
3	32 45.2046	17 07.9530
4	32 45.1800	17 07.6464
5	32 45.2082	17 07.5966
6	32 45.2286	17 07.5792
7	32 45.2478	17 07.6908
8	32 45.2646	17 07.7490
9	32 45.3360	17 07.8120
10	32 45.4722	17 07.8006
11	32 45.4914	17 07.5234
12	32 45.4692	17 07.2324
13	32 45.4044	17 07.0758
14	32 45.3882	17 06.8676
15	32 45.4062	17 06.8448
16	32 45.4086	17 06.7344

34 RABAÇAL - BLUE HAT ASCENT

Wp	N	W
1	32 45.2628	17 07.9980
2	32 45.6372	17 08.0070
3	32 45.6486	17 08.0082
4	32 45.6870	17 08.0646
5	32 45.4692	17 07.2324
6	32 45.4914	17 07.5234
7	32 45.4722	17 07.8006
8	32 45.3360	17 07.8120
9	32 45.2286	17 07.5792
10	32 45.2082	17 07.5966
11	32 45.1800	17 07.6464
12	32 45.2046	17 07.9530

35 THE GARDEN LEVADA (Levada da Ribeira da Janela)

Wp	N	W
1	32 51.1032	17 09.9930
2	32 50.9826	17 10.0242
3	32 50.9562	17 10.0608
4	32 50.7132	17 10.1796
5	32 50.6250	17 10.3476
6	32 50.5536	17 10.3452
7	32 50.4894	17 10.4460
8	32 50.3778	17 10.4166
9	32 50.1798	17 10.5864
10	32 50.1564	17 10.5876
11	32 50.1264	17 10.6692
12	32 49.8834	17 10.5894
13	32 49.8234	17 10.6926
14	32 49.6932	17 10.8708

36 FANAL

Wp	N	W
1	32 48.5448	17 08.4876
2	32 48.7626	17 08.6370
3	32 48.8436	17 08.6724
4	32 48.8862	17 08.7036
5	32 48.9588	17 08.7462
6	32 48.5676	17 08.4684
7	32 48.5292	17 08.4726
8	32 48.4914	17 08.3952
9	32 48.4014	17 08.1444
10	32 48.3564	17 08.0790
11	32 47.8272	17 07.8138
12	32 48.1758	17 08.3640

APPENDIX A: MORE WALKING ON MADEIRA

Madeira is blessed with more walking than can be contained in any one book so our task is rather to decide what to include rather than to, 'find all the walking routes in existence'. The 'find all' idea would be the work of a lifetime, rather like keeping up with the island's ever changing road network. While we would like Walk! Madeira to be comprehensive there is only so much that you can include within 160 pages, so here we present some additional walking for those who wish to explore further.

Shirley Whitehead's Madeira Walks (published by Discovery Walking Guides)
When we find a local walker who can write in a lively style and whose concept of walking agrees with our own, we don't like them to get away, so it was with great pleasure that we met with Shirley Whitehead early in our 2006 research trip. Shirley's walk descriptions are published monthly in the Madeira Times and it was pleasing to offer her a publishing contract to bring her collection of walks together in a DWG book.

As she lives in the unique settlement of **Jardim do Mar**, Shirley's routes concentrate on the western regions of Madeira with only a few duplications of Walk! Madeira routes such as **São Lorenço Peninsula** and **Ribeiro Frio** to **Portela**. Shirley is not yet a GPS user but her knowledge of local history and writing style make Shirley Whitehead's Madeira Walks the obvious companion to Walk! Madeira.

The bits we missed

Our hope was to include a few more routes in Walk! Madeira but the tribulations of David's catching a monstrous cold early in our research curtailed these couple of routes:-

BOA VENTURA

A beautifully laid (and maintained) stone cobbled donkey trail climbing a dramatic cliff is hard to resist. Add in *tipico* refreshments at the end of the climb and a dramatic return, and this 'little' route becomes irresistible (except when weighed down by a heavy cold).

Landscapes of Madeira (7th edition Walk 27b) gives a description from the bus stop in **Boa Ventura**, with a shorter alternative if driving; BUT you can do a far better alternative by using the parking area at the end of a new tarmac lane running down the valley (see map) thus saving you 30 minutes rather boring walking each way as in the Landscapes description.

From the parking area, follow a path seaward to join the donkey trail; you could continue seaward to investigate the ruins of an old mill. Looming over us is the cliff as we turn right (E) to steadily climb the trail, ascending through zigzags before the gradient moderates; some sections have wooden rustic railings but don't trust your safety to these structures; simply use them more as guidelines not to go too near the edge.

Stop to look at the stupendous 'north coast' views as we get higher and then a steady eastward ascent brings us up to pass a house and cultivated plots just before emerging on the ER-101 beside **Snack Bar Arco** (approximately 45 minutes).

Take care on your return as the cobbled trail can be slippery; do not attempt in wet or windy weather.

EXTENSION OF WALK 28, GRASS BRIDGE TO CURRAL DAS FREIRAS

If there's one route we regret missing out on (due to David's bad cold), it's this grand walk through the mountains.

Sitting in **Bar Encumeada** (pre-cold) when the rain was lashing down, we had the route confirmed by a pair of very sodden English walkers who had set out from **Boca da Corrida** in the morning and were awaiting the arrival of the N°139 bus (actually the only bus) back to **Funchal**.

Our choice would be to start at **Encumeada** using the N°139 9.00 a.m. departure from **Funchal** and have coffee in **Bar Encumeada** before setting out.

From the **Green Bridge**, continue on the well-made donkey trail to the trail junction at **Boca do Cerro** (see Madeira Tour & Trail Super-Durable Map published by Discovery Walking Guides) where we can take a decision on whether to tackle **Pico Grande**, depending on the weather and how we felt.

From **Boca do Cerro** you could go south to **Boca da Corrida**, but below the forestry house you face a long downhill trudge down to **Jardim da Serra** and **Corticeiras** to catch the N°80 bus.

Our choice is the shorter though steep descent to **Curral das Freiras** where we find touristy bars and the far more frequent Nº81 Town Bus service back into **Funchal**; the bus ride is an adventure in itself, despite the opening of new tunnels which make it less dramatic.

RIBEIRA DA JANELA - PR15 - PR14 - FANAL

PR15 fingerpost

Madeira's regional government has been spending money on wayposts for some of the island's walking routes including a little known *levada* that almost shadows the new ER-209 road from **Ribeira da Janela** to **Fanal** through one of the least discovered regions of the island. Access is by car with limited roadside car parking at the northern end of the waymarked trail so you might choose to drive up to **Fanal** to walk the combined route 'downhill out - uphill return'.

PR15 is signed off the ER-209 at 32 50.6525N 17 09.3025W with a waypost and the information; 'Curral Falso, 2.7km, 1.5 hours, max altitude 820m, min altitude 400m'.

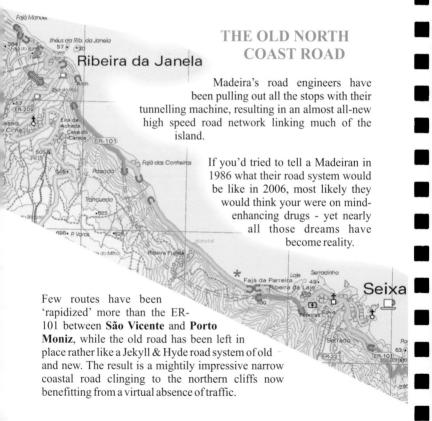

THE OLD NORTH COAST ROAD

Madeira's road engineers have been pulling out all the stops with their tunnelling machine, resulting in an almost all-new high speed road network linking much of the island.

If you'd tried to tell a Madeiran in 1986 what their road system would be like in 2006, most likely they would think your were on mind-enhancing drugs - yet nearly all those dreams have become reality.

Few routes have been 'rapidized' more than the ER-101 between **São Vicente** and **Porto Moniz**, while the old road has been left in place rather like a Jekyll & Hyde road system of old and new. The result is a mightily impressive narrow coastal road clinging to the northern cliffs now benefitting from a virtual absence of traffic.

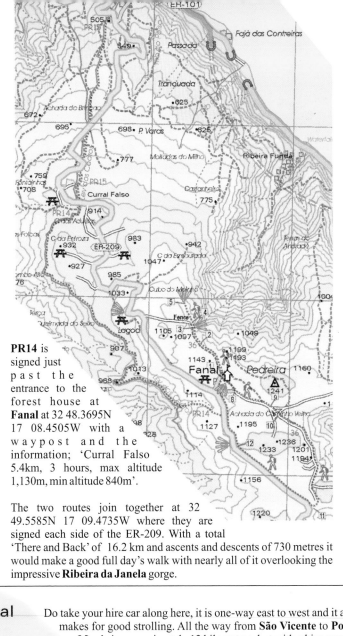

PR14 is signed just past the entrance to the forest house at **Fanal** at 32 48.3695N 17 08.4505W with a waypost and the information; 'Curral Falso 5.4km, 3 hours, max altitude 1,130m, min altitude 840m'.

The two routes join together at 32 49.5585N 17 09.4735W where they are signed each side of the ER-209. With a total 'There and Back' of 16.2 km and ascents and descents of 730 metres it would make a good full day's walk with nearly all of it overlooking the impressive **Ribeira da Janela** gorge.

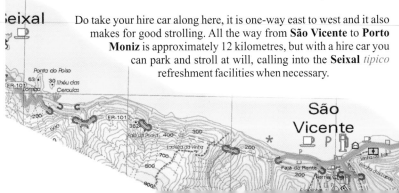

Do take your hire car along here, it is one-way east to west and it also makes for good strolling. All the way from **São Vicente** to **Porto Moniz** is approximately 12 kilometres, but with a hire car you can park and stroll at will, calling into the **Seixal** *tipico* refreshment facilities when necessary.

APPENDIX B: USEFUL INFORMATION

Telephone numbers are shown in red, fax numbers in blue, and email addresses/web sites in green.

Please note that, while the following information is believed to be correct at the time of printing, it is advisable to check on opening hours etc. on arrival. Ask in tourist offices, or your hotel reception staff may be able to help.
The dial code for Madeira when calling from overseas is 00 351.

TAXIS
24 hour service, island-wide 291 741412

Calheta	291 822129	**Gaula**	291 526643
Camacha	291 922185	**Machico**	291 962480
Câmara de Lobos	291 945229		291 962189
	291 942144		291 962220
	291 942407	**Monte**	291 782158
Campanario	291 953601	**Ponta de Sol**	291 972110
Caniçal	291 961989	**Porto da Cruz**	291 562411
Caniço	291 934640	**Porto Moniz**	291 852243
	291934606	**Ribeira Brava**	291 951800
	291 934522		291 952606
Faial	291 572416		291 952349
		Ribeiro Frio	291 782158
Funchal		**Santa Cruz**	291 524888
Central	291 222500		291 524430
Avenida do Mar	291 224588	**Santana**	291 572540
Mercado (market)	291 226400	**Santo da Serra**	291 522100
São Martinho Church	291 765620	**São Vicente**	291 842238
Nazaré	291 762780		

USEFUL PHONE NUMBERS
Emergencies   112
Airport   291 920700
Coastguard   291 763115   291 700112
Police   291 222022
Red Cross (Cruz Vermelha) 291 741115

TOURIST INFORMATION
The regional tourist offices do not always keep to their published opening times, but the main **Funchal** office is reliable. You will find a few leaflets to take away, although most publications need to be purchased.

Please note that some businesses appear to offer unofficial 'tourist information' when there aim is to sell you coah trips, hire cars or time share. The Tourist Offices listed below are the 'official' Madeira Tourist Authority offices.

Main Tourist Office **Funchal**   291 211902   291 232151
Direcção Regional do Turismo   info@madeira tourism.org
Avenida Arriaga N°18   www.madeiratourism.org
9004-519 Funchal
                    Monday - Friday 9.00 a.m. - 8.00 p.m.
                    Saturday - Sunday 9.00 a.m. - 6.00 p.m.

Tourist Office, **Monumental Lido**   291 775254
C.C. Monumental Lido
Estrada Monumental, 284
9000-100 Funchal
> Monday - Friday 9.00 a.m. - 8.00 p.m.
> Saturday 9.00 a.m. - 2.00 p.m.

Tourist Office at the **Airport**   291 524933
Santa Catarina de Baixo
9100 Santa Cruz
> Daily 9.00 a.m. - 12.00 p.m.

Tourist Office, **Caniço**   921 932919
9125 Caniço de Baixo
9100 Santa Cruz
> Monday - Friday 9.00 a.m. - 12.30 p.m. & 2.00 p.m. - 5.30 p.m.

Tourist Office, **Machico**   291 962289
Forte Nossa Senhora do Amparo
9200 Machico
> Monday - Friday 9.00 a.m. - 12.00 p.m.& 2.00 p.m. - 5.00 p.m.
> Saturday 09.30 a.m. - 12.00 p.m.

Tourist Office, **Ribeira Brava**   921 951675
Forte de São Bento
9350 Ribeira Brava
> Monday - Friday 9.00 a.m. - 12.30 p.m. & 2.00 p.m. - 5.00 p.m.
> Saturday 9.30 a.m. - 12.00 p.m.

Tourist Office, **Câmara de Lobos**   921 943470
Town Hall
Câmara de Lobos
Largo de República
9300 Câmara de Lobos
> Monday - Friday 9.00 a.m. - 12.30 p.m. & 2.00 p.m. - 5.00 p.m.
> Saturday 9.30 a.m. - 12.00 p.m.

Tourist Office, **Porto Moniz**   291 850193
Porto Moniz
9270 Porto Moniz
> Monday - Friday 10.00 a.m. - 3.00 p.m.
> Saturday 12.00 p.m. - 3.00 p.m.

Tourist Office, **Santana**   291 572992
Sitio do Serrado
9230 Santana
> Monday - Friday 9.00 a.m. - 12.30 p.m. & 2.00 p.m. - 5.30 p.m.
> Saturday 9.30 a.m. - 12.00 p.m.

Tourist Office, **Porto Santo**   291 982361
Avenida Henrique Vieira e Castro
Porto Santo 9400
> Monday - Friday 9.00 a.m. - 5.30 p.m.
> Saturday 10.00 a.m. - 12.30 p.m.

GARDENS

Check that opening times are still current by visiting the garden websites (where available) or check in the Tourist Information Offices on arrival. Note that most gardens charge a modest entry fee.

Monte Palace Tropical Garden (and museum)   www.montepalace.com
Caminho do Monte
Monte   Open daily 9.30 a.m. to 6 p.m. daily.

Jardim Botânico da Madeira   www.sra.pt/jarbot
Quinta do Bom Sucesso
Funchal   Open daily (not Christmas Day) 9.00 a.m. to 6 p.m.

Quinta das Cruzes (gardens and museum)   www.sra.pt/jarbot/
Calçada de Santa Clara
Funchal   Open Monday to Friday 10.00 a.m. to 17.30 p.m.

Quinta Vigia
Avenida do Infante
Parque de Santa Catarina
Funchal   Monday to Friday 9.00 a.m. to 5 p.m.

Municipal Dona Amélia Garden   www.sra.pt/jarbot
Avenida Arriaga
Funchal

Quinta das Cruces Garden   www.rpmuseus-pt.org
Calçado do Pico
Funchal   Open Tuesday to Sunday 10.00 a.m. to 6 p.m.

Palheiro Gardens   www.madeira-gardens.com
Palheiro Ferreiro   Open Monday to Friday 9.30 a.m. to 12.30 p.m.

Quinta da Boa Vista
Rua do Lombo da Boa Vista
Funchal   Open Monday to Saturday 9.00 a.m. to 5.30 p.m.

Orchid Garden   www.madeiraorchids.com
Rua Pita da Silva
Funchal   Open daily 9.30 a.m. to 6 p.m.

Quinta do Arco Rose Garden   www.quintadoarco.com
Arco de São Jorge   Open daily 11.00 to 6 p.m.

FESTIVALS/ANNUAL EVENTS

For the exact dates when each of these annual events will take place, see www.madeiratourism.org

- Flower Festival 2 day event towards the end of April.
- Carnival mid-February
- Atlantic Festival June
- Wine Festival End August/beginning September
- Festival of the Bands mid-October

GOLF

For general golf information see www.madeiragolf.com

Palheiro Golf   291 792116   291 792456
Quinta do Palheiro Ferreiro   reservations@palheirogolf.com
São Gonçalo   www.palheirogolf.com
9050-296 FUNCHAL

Santo da Serra Golf   reservas@santodaserragolf.com
Machico   www.santodaserragolf.com

HORSE RIDING
Terras de Aventura   291 776818   291 771018
Caminho do Amparo, 25   terrasdeaventura@mail.telepac.pt
9000-248 FUNCHAL   www.madeira-island/aventura

DIVING
Galodiving - Manta Diving Center   291 930930   291 934555
Hotel Galomar - Caniço para a Cidade   stefan@mantadiving.com
9125-031 CANIÇO   www.mantadiving.com

Horizonte do Atlântico   963 390796   291 280024
Rua do Quebra Costas, 28, 2º Dto   venturadomar@iol.pt
9000-034 FUNCHAL   www.venturadomar.com

Leisurelite
Sitio das Eiras, Apartado 76   info@madeira-leisurelite.com
9100-190 SANTA CRUZ   www.madeira-leisurelite.com

Nautisantos   291 231312   291 231312
Marina do Funchal   nautisantos@netmadeira.com
9000-055 FUNCHAL   www.nautisantosfishing.com

Tubarão Madeira Mergulho   291 709227   291 794124
Hotel Pestana Palms, Lido   tubarao.madeira@netmadeira.com
9000-107 FUNCHAL   www.scuba-madeira.com

CLIMBING
Alles   965 012367   291 762003
Estrada Monumental - Hotel Baia Azul
9000-108 FUNCHAL   eduardo.lucas@netmadeira.com

Essência   962 582699
Santa
9270-093 PORTO MONIZ
Terras de Aventura   291 776818   291 771018
Caminho do Amparo, 25   terrasdeaventura@mail.telepac.pt
9000-248 FUNCHAL   www.madeira-island/aventura

SAILING
Alles   965 012367   291 762003
Estrada Monumental - Hotel Baia Azul   eduardo.lucas@netmadeira.com
9000-108 FUNCHAL

Bonita da Madeira "Dream Cruises" 291 762218   291 763545
Estrada Monumental, Ap Baía   info@bonita-da-madeira.com
00-100 FUNCHAL   www.bonita-da-madeira.com

Costa do Sol, Lda 291 224390   291 235735
Marina do Funchal
9000-055 FUNCHAL

Gavião, Viagens Turísticas 291 241124   291 706401
Marina do Funchal   gaviaomadeira@netmadeira.com
9000-055 FUNCHAL

Green Storm 919 996099   291 706401
Rua Santa Luzia, 83 - G   info@greenstorm.pt
9050-068 FUNCHAL   www.greenstorm.pt

Horizonte do Atlântico 963 390796   291 280024
Rua do Quebra Costas, 28, 2º Dto   venturadomar@iol.pt
9000-034 FUNCHAL   www.venturadomar.com

Leisurelite
Sitio das Eiras, Apartado 76   info@madeira-leisurelite.com
9100-190 SANTA CRUZ   www.madeira-leisurelite.com

Lobosonda 963 103762   291 771582
Marina do Lugar de Baixo E21   lobosonda@sapo.pt
9360-119 LUGAR DE BAIXO

Amigos da Natureza 291 220703   291 220703
Rua Portão São Tiago, 19 B   naturfreundemadeira@hotmail.com
9060-250 FUNCHAL   www.naturfreunde-reisen-madeira.com

Prazer do Mar 291 224900 291 224900
Rua do Lazareto, Impasse 1, Casa 5   info@madeiracatamaran.com
9050-365 FUNCHAL   www.madeiracatamaran.com

Pride of Madeira 291 936004 291 93600
Estrada do Garajau, 194   info@prideofmadeira.com
Edif.Qta do Garajau, B1,B5   www.prideofmadeira.com
9125-067 CANIÇO

Santa Maria 291 220327 291 220327
Marina - Funchal   nau.santa.maria@mail.telepac.pt
9000-055 FUNCHAL

StressZero 291 205757   291 205705
Rua Carvalho Araújo, 9   regency@madeiraregency.pt
9000-022 FUNCHAL   www.regency-hotels-resorts.com

Ventura do Mar 291 280033 291 280024
Marina do Funchal, pontão B   venturadomar@iol.pt
9000-055 FUNCHAL

FISHING
Euromar   291 200750   291 229220
Avenida do Infante, 58   sede@euromar-travel.com
9004-526 FUNCHAL

Fish Madeira
Travessa das Virtudes, 23
9000-664 FUNCHAL

291 752685
bristow@netmadeira.com
www.fishmadeira.com

Madeira Big Game Fishing
Marina do Funchal
9000-055 FUNCHAL

291 227169   291 231823
madeira.fishing@clix.pt
www.madeiragamefish.com

Nautisantos
Marina do Funchal
9000-055 FUNCHAL

291 231312   291 231312
nautisantos@netmadeira.com
www.nautisantosfishing.com

Turilobos
Marina do Funchal
9000-055 FUNCHAL

291 238422   291 238422
sportsfishing@mail.telepac.pt

Turimar
Marina do Funchal, Loja 15
9000-055 FUNCHAL

291 226720   291 282175
turimar@netmadeira.com

Turipesca
Marina do Funchal
9000-055 FUNCHAL

291 231063   291 766020
turipesca.fishingcenter.braz@clix.pt

Xiphias Sport Fishing Charters
Marina do Funchal
9000-055 FUNCHAL

291 280007   291 280007
xiphias_charters@yahoo.com
www.geocities.com/xiphias_charters

BIRD WATCHING
Horizonte do Atlântico
Rua do Quebra Costas, 28, 2º Dto
9000-034 FUNCHAL

963 390796   291 280024
venturadomar@iol.pt
www.venturadomar.com

Madeira Wind Birds
Rua da Pena, 10 G
9050-099 FUNCHAL

291 723171
info@madeirabirds.com
www.madeirabirds.com

APPENDIX C: BIBLIOGRAPHY

A search on amazon.co.uk offers over 400 publications - but many are old and difficult to obtain other than as second hand books. Included in the listings are many old maps; some now so out of date as to seem that they hardly relate to modern Madeira at all. Madeira changes rapidly as a result of development and vigorous and ongoing road tunnel programmes, so it makes sense to obtain the most recently researched and published mapping.

MAPS

Madeira Tour & Trail Super-Durable Map (ISBN 1-904946-26-7 £7.99 pub. 2006 Discovery Walking Guides Ltd.).
Our latest 4th Edition, recognised by the 'Yellow Flash' on its cover, is simply the best map of Madeira you can buy at any price. Large 40,000 scale combined with the latest ground survey information, modern design techniques and our incredible Super-Durable material mean that you get both the latest and toughest map available. Nothing else on the market even comes close for value, accuracy, clarity and usability.

Madeira Bus & Touring Map (ISBN 1-904946-09-7 £2.50 pub. 2005 Discovery Walking Guides Ltd.).
Madeira buses are a popular way to see the island and while driving standards have improved (in our opinion) since our earlier visits it is still a harrowing experience to navigate round the island by hire car; possibly not helped by out of date map - see below. Our pocket money Bus & Touring Map is a great way to plan your Madeiran adventures.

All other Madeira Maps.
We look at everything that is on sale when we are on Madeira researching. In May 2006 the situation for island maps for either driving or walking was dire in the extreme! Road systems are changing rapidly, and our Madeira Tour & Trail Map is the only island map that is fully up to date; even our 3rd edition was better than anything else that was on sale. Buying the wrong map can result in a very frustrating holiday, to say nothing of the domestic arguments these awful maps can provoke. Simply buy the best map at £7.99. If you insist on buying a cheaper map then do not complain to us that your 'penny pinching' has ruined your holiday.

WALKING GUIDE BOOKS

Madeira is a walkers' paradise so it comes as a surprise to find almost no locally produced walking guides in the shops compared to other destinations where the shops all seem to have booklets by local walking wanabees. At DWG we are doing our bit to encourage local walkers as **Shirley Whitehead's Madeira Walks** new book shows; complementing our **Walk! Madeira.** We extol the virtues of Shirley's book elsewhere so our only comment here is **BUY**.

Levadas and Footpaths of Madeira by Raimundo Quintal (ISBN 9-729177-18-X pub. 1999)
Looks interesting on a shop's shelf, but this book falls down as soon as you try to use it; no contents list and no index mean you spend endless time trying to find the walk description you want. When we've tried routes from this book, we've found the descriptions lacking in almost everything; poor directions, no times, no compass directions etc. This book could have been so much better if only Raimundo would learn book design and what walkers' want in a route description. He has not moved on since 1999 and his new book on the shelves shows all the

same short comings of this title. Verdict: Leave it on the shelf.

Landscapes of Madeira by John & Pat Underwood (ISBN 1-856912-64-7 pub. 2005 £10.99)

All English speaking walkers on Madeira owe a big debt to Pat & John for introducing us to the island through their first edition way back in the 1980s, and winner of the Thomas Cook Travel Book award when first published. Pat & John were on Madeira at the same time as us (May 2006) and it would have been good if we had bumped into each other to swop experiences. They tend to concentrate more on the vertiginous than we do, so if you have a head for heights this could be for you. You can print off the latest route updates from their website; useful if you already have an earlier edition. Map sections are a lot better now that John draws the maps himself. If we have criticisms of the Landscapes series it's that while the covers change with new editions the content is little changed, and that quite a lot of each book (40% or so) is taken up with generalist advice when we feel that more attention could be given to each walking route's description. Verdict: If you are looking for an alternative to DWG books then buy this, by far the best of the competition.

Madeira Walk & Eat by John & Pat Underwood (pub. 2005 £6.99)

A sort of cut-down Landscapes but with emphasis on cuisine added. Far fewer walks than the Landscapes book but if you want to know how to cook what you have been eating this could be the alternative to J&P's main walking book. Have they hit the 'bull' for a new gourmet walking market? We think not, as there are better walking books (including their own) and probably more in depth cuisine books, so looks as if this series is designed for the impulse ambling market. Verdict; possible buy if you don't want to do much walking.

Madeira Rother Walking Guide translated from the German (pub.Rother ISBN 3-763348-11-5 2001 £8.99)

Rother have translated their attractive series of red covered, pocket sized books into an English series. Having quite a lot of these on our shelves for various destinations in both English and German, our criticism is that while they are attractive when browsing, in practice we find the descriptions 'cropped' to fit a set number of pages, mapping is average, and the English translation can leave something to be desired. Photos are over-sized and would be better if reduced in size thus allowing more space for more detailed walk description. Good size to put in your pocket. Verdict: Better on the shelf than in our pocket.

Walking in Madeira by Paddy Dillon (ISBN 1-852843-34-9 pub. 2001 £12.00)

We've not bothered to buy a copy of Paddy's book because we were so disappointed by his two books covering the Canary Islands; awful mapping, no timings, no compass directions, rather pointless starts and finishes giving access or return problems etc. Assuming that Paddy has treated Madeira in the same manner and if we cannot say something good then say nothing at all; nothing.

REFERENCE BOOKS

Madeira: Plants and Flowers by Antonio Da Costa
(£47.56Hardcover Pub.: Vaxter Och Blommor ISBN 9-729177-13-9)

Flores da Madeira by Rui Vieira
(£8.97 280 pages Pub. 1986 Francisco Ribeiro ISBN B0000EHHMX

Flora of Madeira by M.J. Short
(pub. 2001 J.R. Press £32.00 572 pages (September 1, 2001) ISBN 1-898298-80-7

Prion Birdwatchers' Guide to Portugal and Madeira by H. Costa, C.C. Moore, G. Elias(pub. Prion Birdwatchers' Guide)

Field Guide to the Birds of the Atlantic Islands: Canary Islands, Madeira, Azores, Cape Verde by Tony Clarke, Chris Orgill (Illustrator), Tony Disley (£23.74 320 pages Pub.2006 Christopher Helm Publishers Ltd ISBN: 0-713660-23-6)

GENERAL GUIDES

Compared to the specialist walking guide books we find these 'general' guides rather old fashioned. Surely there must be a better way of presenting what is basically a list of 'well known' things to do backed up by 'where to shop' and 'where to eat' sections; often giving the impression (hopefully false) that the businesses pay to be in the guide, rather like yellow pages. Style of general guide books still seems geared to a fast disappearing tourist age possibly now only holding out amongst cruise-tourists.

Most popular of general Madeira guide books on Amazon, though all titles are generally less popular than the specialist walking guide books and maps, are:

Rough Guide Madeira	(published 2005 £6.99)
AA Spiral Guide Madeira	(published 2002 £9.99)
Eyewitness Madeira	(published 2005 £6.99)
AA Essential Madeira	(published 2005 £5.99)
Insight Guide Madeira	(published 2002 £16.99)
Berlitz Pocket Guide Madeira	(published 2004 £4.99)

If you are looking for a general guide you could try shopping in Matalan - yes the clothes and household discount stores, where we noticed AA guides at 1/3rd of their published price, or The Works remainder book shops where you can often find general guide book titles at a 1/3rd of their original price. These are usually, but not always, for the previous edition but might offer better value than buying the current edition at full price.

LOCAL NEWSPAPERS AND MAGAZINES IN ENGLISH

Picking up a local paper or magazine can quickly give an insight to island life. On Madeira this falls to **The Madeira Times** monthly newspaper and **Madeira Island Bulletin** bimonthly magazine. Both publications tend towards the modest but are freely available from the piles found in hotel receptions and outside advertisers premises. Rather thin on content, with the exception of Shirley Whitehead's walking article in the Times, both act as an outlet for advertisers first and wanabee columnists second; criticism of any aspect of the island is conspicuous by its absence!

Local English Radio & TV Stations
None.

The network of bus services around Madeira is remarkable. The buses are cheap, usually punctual and are a fun way to see the island and to reach and return from some walking routes.

However, finding out which bus you need can be confusing, to say the least; this is because several operators run public bus services, and sometimes use the same bus numbers for entirely different routes.

Timetable changes happen quite frequently, so use our bus information solely as a guide. Pick up the latest bus numbers and times when you get to Madeira from tourist offices, and from the little information/ticket kiosks which you find along the main **Avenida do Mar**. You will find that most of the main bus stops are spread along this *avenida*, or in the adjoining streets.

The main bus operator for the **Funchal** region is Horários do Funchal, offering about fifty routes. They have a special cheap seven day ticket for a week of travel on their routes. Operators of out of town and country routes include SAM, Rodoeste, and EAC.

To get the very best out of Madeira's bus services, arm yourself with the Madeira Bus & Touring Map (pub. Discovery Walking Guides Ltd. 1-904946-09-7 £2.50) which includes details of all the routes, itineraries, timetables and more.

ORANGE TOWN BUSES SERVE THE FOLLOWING DESTINATIONS:

Orange (town) buses serve the following destinations:

N°1	Ponta da Laranjeira
N°2	Papagaio Verde
N°3	Lombada
N°4	Pico dos Barcelos
N°5	Lido
N°7	Travessa do Pomar
N°8	Santa Quitéria (via Barreiros)
N°8A	Santa Quitéria
N°9	Courelas
N°10	Chamorra
N°11	Trapiche
N°12	Jamboto (via Hospital)
N°13	Jamboto (via Viveiros)
N°14	Álamos
N°15	Santana
N°15A	Achada
N°16	Santa Quitéria
N°16A	Pinheiro das Voltas
N°17	Lombo Segundo
N°18	São João
N°19	Levada da Corujeira (via Pena)
N°19	Levada da Corujeira (via Til)
N°20	Monte (via Corujeira de Dentro)
N°21	Monte (via Largo da Fonte)
N°22	Babosas
N°23	Livramento
N°24	Pizo (industrial zone)
N°25	Levada de Santa Luzia (via Til)
N°26	Levada de Santa Luzia (via Pena)
N°27	Caminho de Ferro
N°28	Dr. João
N°29	Curral dos Romeiros
N°30	Largo do Miranda
N°31	Jardim Botánico
N°32	Rochinha
N°33	Balancal
N°34	Canto do Muro
N°34A	Caminho do Pasto
N°35	Praia Formosa
N°36	Lombo da Quinta
N°37	Palheiro Ferreiro
N°38	Cancela
N°39	Montanha
N°40	Quinta da Rocha
N°42	Alegria
N°43	Romeiras
N°44	Nazaré (via Virtudes)
N°45	Nazaré (via Barreiros)
N°46	Ribeira Grande
N°47	São João Latrão

Route of Orange Town Bus Nº48

We give a special mention for this useful and interesting Town Bus as it is oddly missing from many official timetables. It serves many tourist apartments and hotels as well as accessing our walks numbers 2, 3 and 5.

Nazare - C do Engelo Velo - Madie Bell - Capella do Amparo - Apt America - Apt Poirnais - Hotel Madeira Palacio - Corana - Hotel Dues Torres - Hotel Baia Azul - Hotel Alto Lido - Lido Sol - CZ Lido - Hotel Cliff Bay - Reids Hotel - Freitas & Netto - Hospital Cruz Carvalho - Est Horacio Vento Gorvasio - Vertudes - Rua das Vertudes - C das Vertudes - Apt das Vertudes - Aviata Navia - Turegardo Sao Marinho - Hyper SA - São Martinho - C Esmerelda - Quinta Esmerelda - Before Pavirao Trabaladores - Pavilao dos Trabaladores - Miradouro Pico dos Barcellos - Estacio dio Madeira - Rem Mira - Romeiros - Rua William Edward Clod - Porto Medico - Depors Porto Medico - Igreje Santo Antonio - C da Igregia - C Allemana - Barranco Allemans - Casa de Saida de Pentende - Apt de Pentende - C de Agua de Mel - Prix de Agua de Mel - C de Agua de Mel - After Super Rayo Roque - Punta de Freg de Rayo Roque - Fedora de Siema - Antiga Pedre Eira de Cima - C dos Saltos - Mira Funda de Cima - Estacion dos Mar Meldros - Rua 1st Mayo - before do Miradouro Mar Meldros - Ent Sanatorio Hospital dos Marmaleros - Tanque Monte - Universidad de Monte - before Largo da Font - Monte Largo de Font.

COUNTRY BUSES BY COLOUR
From/To Funchal

BUS COMPANY	COLOUR(S)
RODOESTE	CREAM/RED
SA DO CURRAL	CREAM/BLUE
SAM	CREAM/GREEN
EACL	GREY/RED
ECCL	CREAM/BLUE
SR DO FAIAL	CREAM/RED

Route Numbers and Destinations (from **Funchal**)

Nº2 Assomada		Nº96 Corticeiras	
Nº3 Estreito de Câmara de Lobos		Nº103 Boaventura	
Nº4 Madalena do Mar		Nº107 Ponta do Pargo	
Nº6 Boaventura		Nº110 Noguiera	
Nº7 Ribeira Brava		Nº113 Machico, Caniçal	
Nº20 Santo da Serra		Nº114 Noguiera	
Nº23 Machico		Nº115 Estreito da Calheta	
Nº25 Santo da Serra		Nº123 Campanário	
Nº29 Camacha		Nº138 São Jorge	
Nº53 Faial		Nº139 Porto Moniz	
Nº60 Boqueirão		Nº142 Ponta do Pargo	
Nº77 Santo da Serra		Nº148 Boa Morte	
Nº78 Machico, Faial		Nº154 Cabo Girão	
Nº81 Curral das Freiras		Nº155 Ponta da Oliveira	
		Nº156 Machico, Maroços	

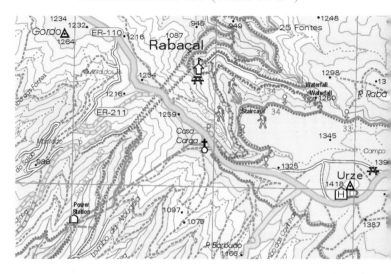

If you haven't been to Madeira for a while, then as you approach **Rabaçal** from the ER-110 road you will, to borrow from the nursery rhyme, be 'in for a big surprise, for all the cars that ever there was are parking now upon the grass because the access road is now closed to private vehicles'. No longer is the descent down to **Rabaçal**, or the ascent back from **Rabaçal**, a potential duel with hire cars coming the opposite way. No more scrimmaging with other hire car drivers trying to find the last space in the large car park; large but never quite large enough. Enough of these now unnecessary tests of machismo driving skill, for now we park all over the meadows alongside the main road; a truly surreal sight after driving through the unpopulated vastness of the **Paul do Serra**.

For those who prefer the steep ride down to **Rabaçal**, or the seemingly steeper climb back up, there is a shuttle mini-bus service. Fares are 2 euros single or 3 euros for a return, and judging by the numbers choosing to ride this is clearly a pleasantly profitable business for the bus operator - with the highest bus fares on Madeira!

The new shuttle-bus system has also increased the number of walkers using the **Rabaçal - Calheta Tunnel** for access to the **Rabaçal** walking routes. From the ER-110 take the ER-211 narrow tarmac lane for approximately two kilometres and then park opposite the track for the **Rabaçal - Calheta Tunnel**; currently there is adequate parking by an old ruin. A twelve minute stroll brings us to the tunnel and in another twenty minutes we emerge from the large tunnel onto a beautiful section of the **Levada das 25 Fontes** - quite the best way of arriving in **Rabaçal**.

GLOSSARY

This glossary lists Portuguese words used in the text and shown in *purple italics*, plus some other local words you may encounter.

A
achada	plateau		channel
aeroporto	airport	*lombada*	mountain ridge
água	water	**M**	
alto	high	*mar*	sea
autocarro	bus	*mercado*	market
B		*miradouro*	viewing point
baía	bay	*monte*	mountain
baixo	low	**P**	
bica	spring	*palheiro*	thatched cottage or animal shelter
boca	pass (in mountains)	*palmeira*	palm
C		*paragem*	bus stop
caldeirão	cauldron shaped crater or rock basin	*pastelaria*	cake shop
		paúl	marshland
caminho	path, country road	*penha*	cliff, ridge
campo	field, plain	*pico*	peak (mountain)
caniço	reed	*poço*	well
centro de saúde	medical centre	*poio*	agricultural terrace
choupana	hut, cottage	*pomar*	orchard
cima	above	*ponte*	bridge
correios	post office	*porto*	port
cova	cavern	*posto florestal*	forest house
cruz	cross	*pousada*	hotel (government run)
curral	animal pen	**Q**	
E		*quebrada*	steep slope, ravine
estrada	road	*quinta*	farm house, country manor
F		**R**	
faial	beech trees	*ribeira*	river
fonte	spring	*risco*	danger
furado	levada tunnel	**S**	
G		*serra*	mountain range
gaviota	gull	*sol*	sun
I		**T**	
ilhéu	island	*teleférico*	cable car
J		*torre*	tower
jardim	garden	**V**	
L		*vale*	valley
lago/lagoa	lake, pool		
lamaceiros	marsh land		
levada	aqueduct, water		

Walk! Wire-O Spiral Bound Guidebooks are designed to be used with:

- DWG's plastic slipcover (PSC), which prevents the binding from catching on pockets and increases durability -
- - and our clear plastic All Weather Book Bag (AWBB) with grip-top seal which allows the book to be folded back displaying 2 pages, then sealed, impervious to weather conditions.

To obtain your PSC and AWBB for this book, send a C5 (9 x 7 inch) SAE with 50p stamp, to:

(Code 9781904946240)
Discovery Walking Guides
10 Tennyson Close
Northampton NN5 7HJ